Dror
Dreams

Dror
Dreams

Design Without Boundaries

Dror Benshetrit
Foreword by Aric Chen

The Monacelli Press

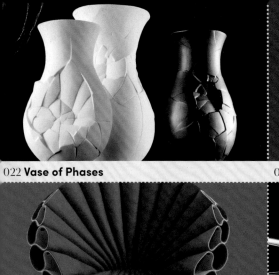

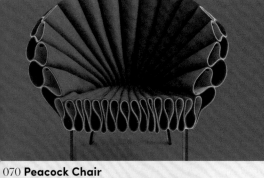

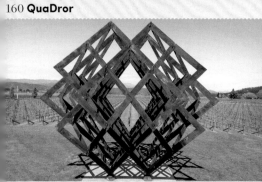

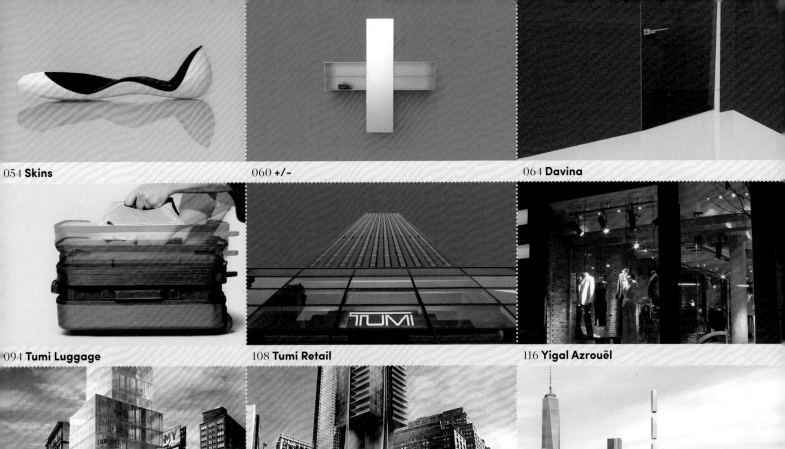

Foreword

Aric Chen

At some point in 2017, Dror Benshetrit decided he wanted to design the moon—and bring it back to Earth. This was not some scheme to tap the celestial body's mineral riches, nor was it a back-up plan for a species well on its way to making its home planet uninhabitable. Neither did it have anything to do with the plutocrats hankering for seats on a future SpaceX or Virgin Galactic flight; in fact, it wasn't really about space travel, or even the moon, at all.

In 1968, Apollo 8 gave humanity its first photo-graphic glimpses of our planet, making the Earth's finite, fragile beauty all too real, and helping to spur the environmental movement. Now, half a century later, Dror's ambition was to create an immersive moon simulation, here on *terra firma,* that might similarly offer a view back onto Earth. Writing in *Surface* magazine, he described his proposal, called Lookback, as a way to "learn to be more respectful toward our planet and actually save this place."

As a designer, Dror has always been drawn to, dare we say, moonshot projects. From his early work transforming clumps of secondhand fur into elegant porcelain jewelry, to more recent projects—an island of architectural "green carpets" in the Persian Gulf, the retractable, 1.2 kilometer long boardwalk of a kinetic cruise ship terminal in Istanbul—he conjures ideas that might sound audacious, fanciful, and even naïve until they come to fruition, as they often do. It's not for nothing that Dror describes himself as a dreamer—but he is a dreamer in the lucid sense, conscious of design's humanistic imperatives and its ability to shape the world for the better.

Originally from Israel, Dror studied at the Design Academy Eindhoven in the Netherlands. Then under the direction of Lidewij Edelkoort, the Dutch trend forecaster known for her shaman-like prophecies, the school's conceptually driven environment steered the young designer towards an approach that imbues objects with narratives, and narratives with meaning, while taking nothing as given.

The Vase of Phases, produced by Rosenthal in 2005, was his first commercially marketed project. Dror had just arrived in New York, where he'd set up a studio in a borrowed basement space beneath his uncle's fashion boutique in the Meatpacking District. It was there, while pondering the seemingly perfect, unblemished forms of porcelain vases, that he took to smashing them. Cracked and deformed, the Vase of Phases series was cast from these broken originals, their shattered silhouettes representing for Dror not just his own vulnerabilities as a young designer, new to both the city and profession, but more broadly, the brittleness of an unpredictable world.

Since then, Dror has channeled those early reflections on uncertainty and fragility into an embrace of change and transformation. With an economy of gestures, he very literally gives movement to form and form to movement: A medicine cabinet becomes simultaneously open and closed with a swift swing of its mirror.

A house mechanically changes with the seasons. A waterfront building peels off from the shoreline, while a dredging project becomes an artificial mountain that sprouts a new kind of city.

It's a diverse body of work. But as with trend forecasting (he briefly assisted Edelkoort in her Paris office), Dror picks up on cues, references, and other scattered bits of information and, through seemingly free associative patterns of thinking, weaves them together—much like dreams. To hear the story behind his wildly successful Peacock chair—which starts with his break-up with a girlfriend and ends with seating made of folded felt, by way of ruminations on dance, Yves Klein, and ornithology—is to begin to understand how broken vases, expandable luggage, kinetic cruise terminals, and artificial moons might make sense within a single designer's output.

Indeed, thinking and working across scales and typologies, Dror gives simple principles shape-shifting complexity in a completely unconstrained way. Consider his QuaDror system. Prompted by a brief from Swarovski, it began as an attempt to reimagine chandeliers. But before long, the simple system he devised—a folding frame of two quasi-parallelograms hinged together—mutated into a cavalcade of iterations: as table legs and shelf supports, folding screens and bottle holders, lighting, and even clothing racks. Milled in wood, cast in concrete, punched from sheet metal, and 3D-printed, proposals for QuaDror-based freeway overpasses, collapsible pavilions, and even highrises soon followed.

Dror's unrelenting devotion to QuaDror, and his belief in its near total applicability—its limitless potential to tackle design problems large and small—might lead one to think of the visionary engineer, designer, and theorist Buckminster Fuller. The latter's almost spiritual faith in human ingenuity, and its capacity to resolve the conundrum of an ever expanding species on a finite planet, manifested in a radically simple geometry of "tensegrity"—the structural principle of the geodesic dome—to which QuaDror could look as a precursor.

And like Fuller, technology for Dror is only valuable to the extent that it becomes "synergetic"—to borrow Fuller's term—with humans and nature. It seems only natural, then, that as this book goes to print, Dror is embarking on a new phase of his life and work as he joins the We Company as cofounder of its future cities initiative. In this role, he'll be leading teams of designers, engineers, scientists, and others to "fuse nature, design, technology, and community in our cities in order to measurably improve the lives of citizens." It's a description that no doubt understates the scope of Dror's hopes and ambitions.

Dror's optimism and idealism make him a designer in the truest sense. To contemplate the more poetic aspects of his work is to engage in a kind of metaphysical meandering. Yet there is also something reassuringly tangible, nuts-and-bolts—and hence intuitive—about his designs. They share a sense of wonderment, if even in the most innocent way. Indeed, Dror's work provokes the imagination. And that remains true whether you're looking at a vase or the moon here on what Fuller famously called "Spaceship Earth."

Introduction

Throughout the years, I have always grappled with the answer to that common question: "So, what do you do?" It has always been difficult to define myself. Similarly, defining our studio practice and the work we do has been an ongoing and evolving challenge for us. How can we sum it up? How can we encapsulate the breadth of our work and ideas in one or two sentences?

I've always been devoted to creativity, to under-standing creative human potential, and to investigating the power of ideas. In observing the natural themes of our work from the last seventeen years, I found that central to what we do is to rethink typologies and structures, finding new ways to improve well-being and create meaningful connection.

We never fit into the traditional boxes of the design industry. Naturally, most of the clients in the industry are looking for a safe and specialized design team with a reputation for delivering the kind of thing that they are looking for. There are design studios that choose one area or one typology to focus on and hone their specialty to make a name for themselves in association with that product. This way of working had never appealed to me. Studio Dror's strength is in *designing without boundaries.*

When we develop a proposal we are compelled to look at it through a holistic lens, examine the possibilities *beyond* the brief. Often we return to the client to suggest a mutation, expansion, or evolution of the project's parameters. We've found clients who are willing to take the risks, to go to a new place with us, and the results have been thrilling and meaningful. But overall I find the service-oriented model of design and architecture is flawed, as it places restraints on the creativity that emerges when artists and designers are given freedom to experiment.

As a result, we have always invested in our own ideas. I find inspiration across all of the industries we have been fortunate to explore, and I have consistently found that our best ideas emerge from unexpected places. To truly innovate you must consider everything, which is why I strongly believe in a comprehensive approach. At Studio Dror we value the holistic power of design and the need to think creatively across disciplines, and we consistently work together with experts and specialists to achieve our dreams.

We as a studio have taken a different approach to being a design service provider, and have invested every spare moment away from client projects to develop our vision and concepts for disruptive ideas, new typologies and inventions. It is not a model I would recommend to anyone seeking a consistent and stable lifestyle, but for me I found great fulfillment in exploring ideas with the team and working to develop game-changing IP, worldwide patents, products, and partnerships. When you take the risks for what you believe in, amazing things can happen. When you approach a client with a novel, unexpected proposal, as opposed to responding to a brief or design competition, it changes the conversation. Through this combination of inspiring client projects and self-initiated endeavors, my true focus and life mission surfaced.

In January 2017, a few months before I'd turn 40, a time when I was entrenched in the challenges of pushing innovation as a design practice servicing clients, I asked myself this question:

What is the most important change I want to see in the world?

The artificial division between the built environment and nature was the first thing I thought about. We must rethink urbanization, we can't keep excavating and clogging our planet with concrete.

As I took myself through this evaluation, I felt a surge of energy output and spent the whole day writing. It was then that I made a conscious decision to commit to working on projects that:
· Consider well-being comprehensively.
· Raise awareness around responsible consumption.
· Create stronger connections between people and their products, between people and the urban environment, people and nature, and between people and other people.

I also realized that when our intentions are guided by love and not need or fear—or even fulfilling a brief—the result is so much more powerful. What if we can elevate that to a place where every project puts life as a whole in its core mission and is driven by the need to improve people's well-being while protecting our planet: keep our valuable natural resources, slow our consumption, elevate the quality of goods, make our cities greener, and integrate architecture into nature instead of replacing nature. As we are part of nature, let's create structures that do not take away from the beauty of nature, but respect it and learn from it.

Now, in addition to the comprehensive design practice at Studio Dror, we have created Supernature Labs, where we turn our focus on connecting cities with nature, introducing new models that can create a symbiotic relationship between urbanism and nature: a new type of urban ecosystem that is a catalyst for change around the world.

This mega-shift toward living in harmony between nature and communities in the twenty-first century marks a massive turning point for my studio, my practice, and my life path. It is the culmination of Studio Dror's past work, and this mission is a direct result of these questions I asked myself.

Dror Dreams chronicles the foundation of my studio practice, and follows the genesis of ideas throughout the first period of our work up to 2018. This book explores how we think about ideas and how they tie into designing for well-being. These are the building blocks toward Dror 2.0. In sharing the stories of *Dror Dreams*, my hope is that the philosophies of idea-creation included here lead others to their own innovations.

With love,

Studio Dror

I will start very generally with four points—pillars—that have emerged in our practice. These are beliefs that shape our work and that we also use to describe how we work.

First, Studio Dror starts as an ideas-driven design practice. I'm extremely passionate about ideas. Ideas are always the starting point, not design.

Design for us always follows a certain approach, a certain ideology, a certain way of thinking. Often, ideas have core meaning, core significance; they are the fundamentals we start with. Authenticity is crucial; we have to believe in everything we do. We want to do more than disrupt: we want to use ideas as a medium to create meaningful connections. As I see it, the role of a designer is to improve well-being.

Second is the holistic approach to design. There is massive significance in a holistic core concept. Everything is connected; everything is relevant. True innovation comes when you consider everything, so I believe it helps that we are a holistic practice that has no boundaries between the disciplines of design. One thing I'd like to say is that design is everything that people have ever created—anything that nature has not. I believe that we are transformable beings desiring transformable objects, environments, and experiences. Why should we create the boundaries of disciplines?

Third is that we're always collaborating. If we are generalists, we always need knowledge, we always seek the best knowledge and the best specialists to support us, make our dreams into reality, and shape our dreams with us. We could never succeed without their incredible contributions, valuable input, and understanding of our desires. We never underestimate the power of the collaborative process. It enhances our ideas with imperative knowledge, experience, and expertise, so we always want to do things with others and not exist in a vacuum. Together, we exchange and evolve.

And fourth, the process is extremely important. The process is always driven by love and not fear or constraints. What I mean by that is that I like to change a lot of words to the word *love*—particularly the word *sustainability*. In many ways, I think one

of the most sustainable things you can do is to make meaningful connections. Between people and objects. Between people and environments. Between people and their city.

I think love is one of the most important things. Beloved objects are passed between generations of family and friends. You don't easily throw away things that you love. When you have a connection to them, things are less disposable.

Chapter 1

Vase of Phases

How can we celebrate the beauty of experience?

When I moved to New York, I always thought to myself that it felt as if I were pregnant. I became pregnant with ideas and started calling myself "we." Even though I was all by myself, I pretended that there was a studio, there was a practice and I had all kinds of people doing different things. It was pretty much just me for a little while, until people

started reaching out asking if they could come and do an internship with me and I would say, "Well yes, but I feel like I'm still interning with myself."

Starting my own practice was not as easy as I thought it was going to be. At some point I felt like I was living a double life. Like, I'm not really sure how I'm going to finish the month and do what I do, and how can I get to do everything that I want to do creatively. At the same time, I was meeting with very important people who had the ability to accelerate my career. I was pretending as if everything was wonderful, but I felt a bit broken. I felt a bit like I was losing my naïveté in many ways—a young kid who had never lived in a big city, moving to New York thinking that he's going to change the American market overnight. To cope, I decided to make something to capture that feeling and that encapsulated this formative experience that New York gives.

I needed to work on that very specific feeling. I thought about objects that symbolized my 25-year-old self—innocent—and saw corresponding qualities in a classic porcelain vase. The worst possible thing that can happen to a vase, I reasoned, is for it to fall and shatter, and that's the end of its life cycle. But that's not the case with us humans. In our lives, we pick ourselves up, we learn from our failures, and they become the things that shape us. As a flower grows within broken soil, the human spirit is shaped by hardship. These episodes often occur when we least expect them, forcing us onto a challenging path that is, in fact, precisely where we're meant to be.

How could breakage become the vessel's defining feature? I started really loving the idea of highlighting

the beauty of the experiences I take myself through and become the experiences that shape me into who I am. I wanted to capture that process in a product.

The first step was to take a simple vase and break it. I began busting a lot of vases. After discovering the time-consuming effort of putting the pieces back together, I lined the interior of one with silicone rubber to keep the pieces in place upon impact. I then dipped the vessel into liquid porcelain to fill in the cracks.

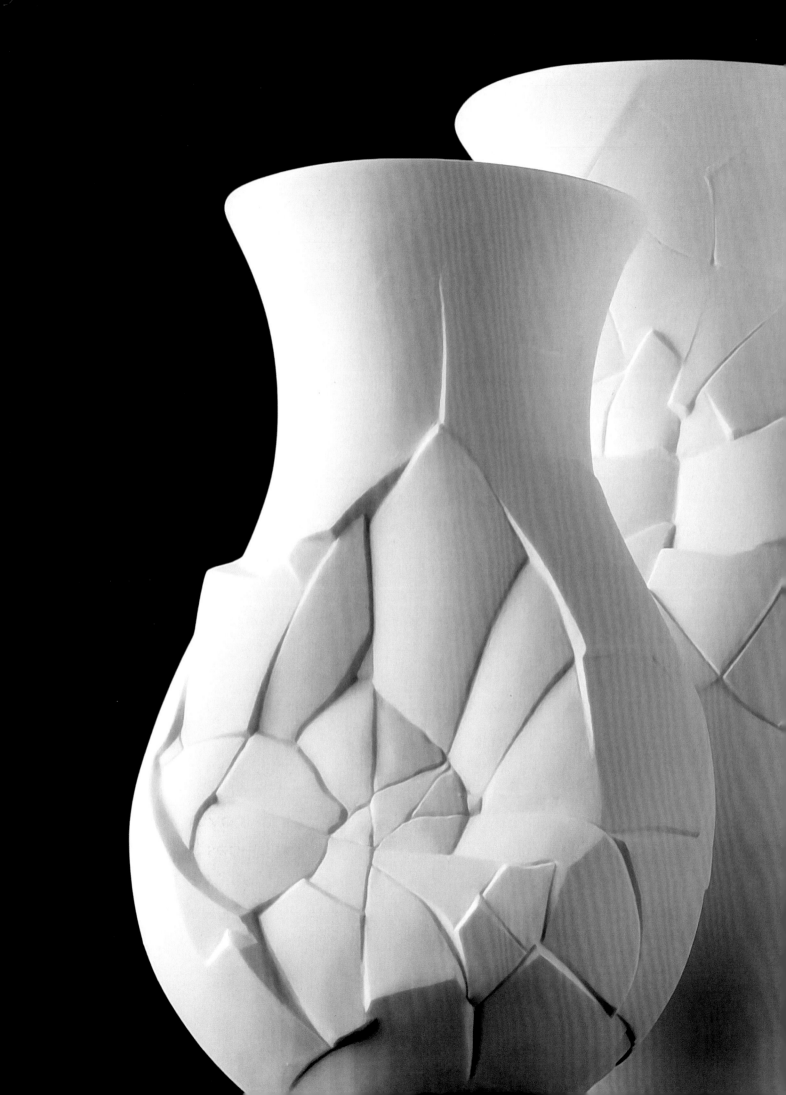

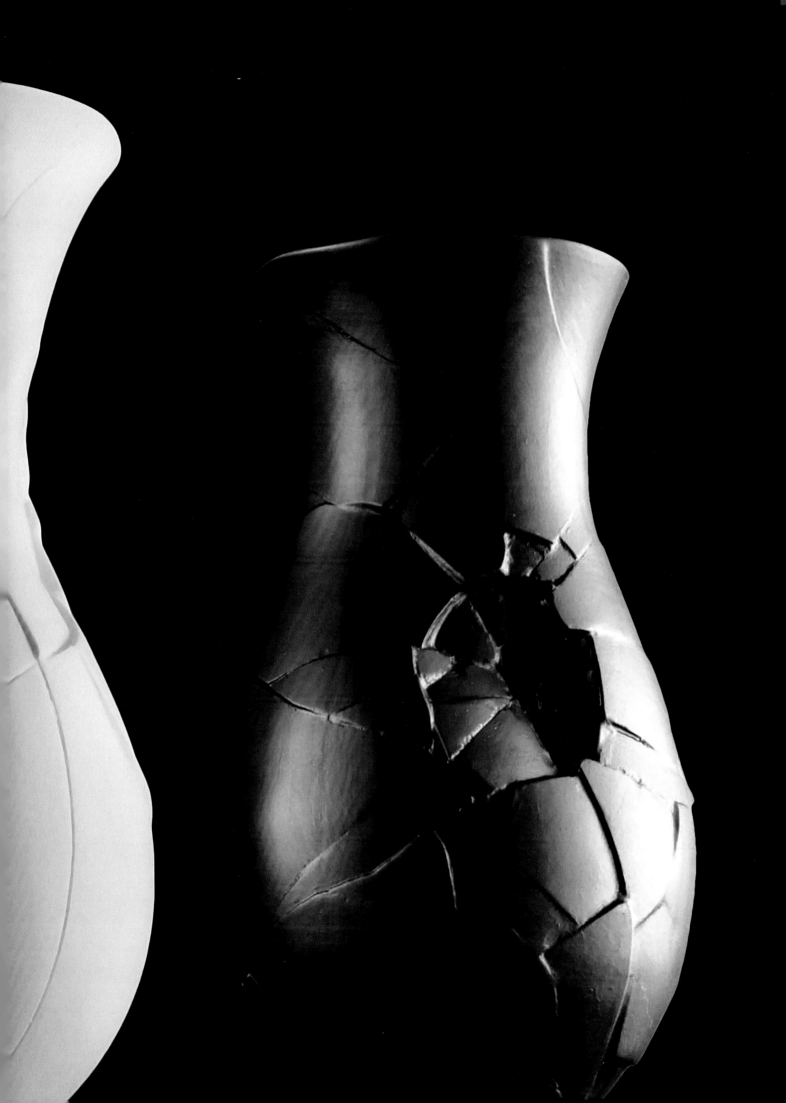

We called it the Vase of Phases. It's a tongue-in-cheek reference to the object's faceted form and the multiple stages of its production process. We produced it ourselves in the practice—we just didn't know how to approach large manufacturers at the time. We said, "Let's just make it ourselves" and bought a kiln. We produced a limited edition run of 200 pieces and packaged them for sale.

Interestingly, this project offered lessons and growth for us aside from the production and techniques

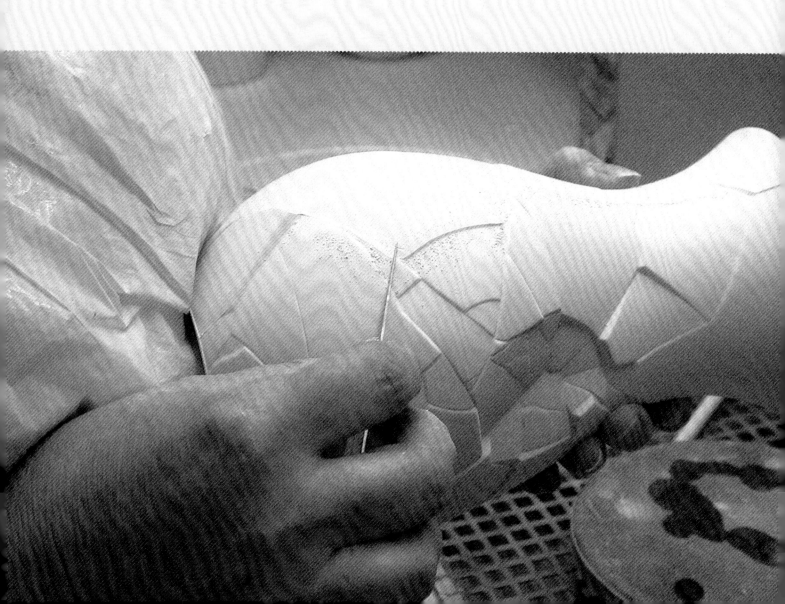

we learned. One day we got a phone call from a stockist carrying our vase. She said, "I'm sorry we're no longer going to carry this product here. Somebody came in and was extremely upset about the message on the packaging of this vase, and we need to take it out." I said, "What do you mean? What's wrong with the message of the vase?" and she said, "Yes, you know it talks about physical abuse and the ability to keep containing water. It talks about virginity and..." And I said, "Wow, wow, wow. The vase is supposed to be me, and it's really

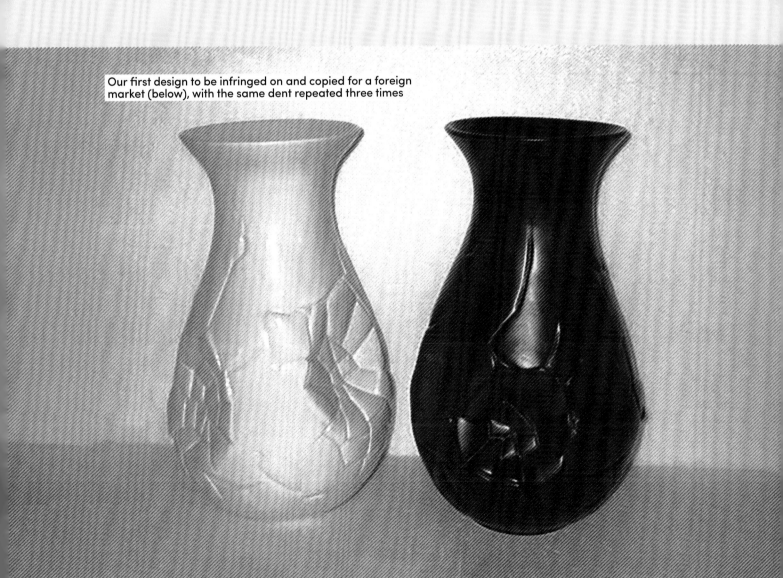

Our first design to be infringed on and copied for a foreign market (below), with the same dent repeated three times

Karl Lagerfeld photographing
the Rosenthal collection by Dror

an analogy of my own life." This was really the first
time I'd realized the importance of everything that
we put out there associated with our projects—down
to the marketing copy. When I read the text on the
packaging again, I could see what she meant, I
could see how it was being interpreted. We wanted
to highlight resilience of the human spirit, and
how transformation can create beauty, but we
needed to explain the concept more clearly. So
of course, we took all the labels out, we wrote the
copy differently and put them back in stores.

Later we presented the vase to Rosenthal and their first reaction was, "We've been trying to perfect porcelain for 125 years and here he comes and highlights the beauty of the imperfection." Which is really the essence of what I tried to create.

One of the things that was really interesting in regards to the success of this product: this was our very first product in the marketplace. It became an icon for Rosenthal. It has been Rosenthal's bestseller in the gift category for many, many years. The Vase of Phases has also been included in museum exhibitions and permanent collections.

When introducing people to our practice, I always start with this product for a couple of reasons: First, it's the easiest way to describe metaphorical transformation. We always talk about transformation as one of the biggest themes in what we do. The second thing is that everybody can relate to it in their own way.

Chapter 2

Pick Chair

Why entertain guests with unsightly chairs that need to be hidden away?

If Vase of Phases represents a metaphorical transformation, the Pick Chair is the product that best
describes physical transformation. This chair was
also my graduation project at the Design Academy
of Eindhoven. I was really fascinated by folding
chairs at the time. Why do people use folding
chairs at home? The primary reason is that you

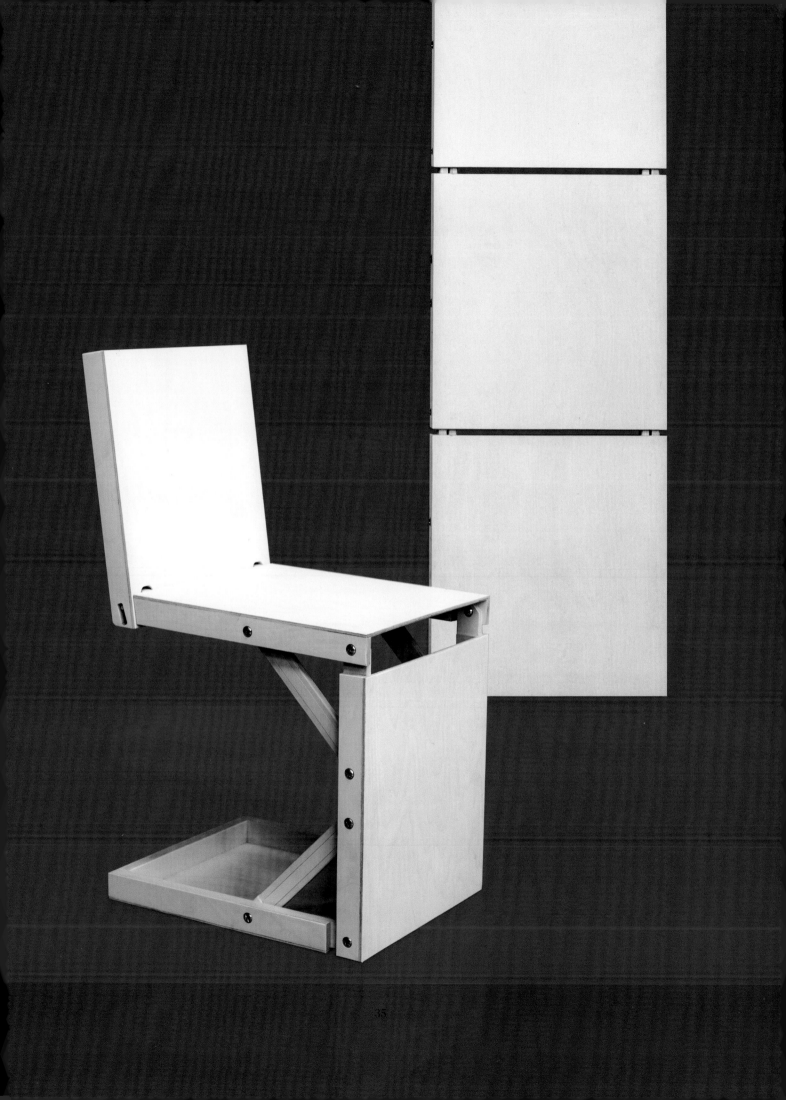

From two-dimensional art to three-dimensional product.

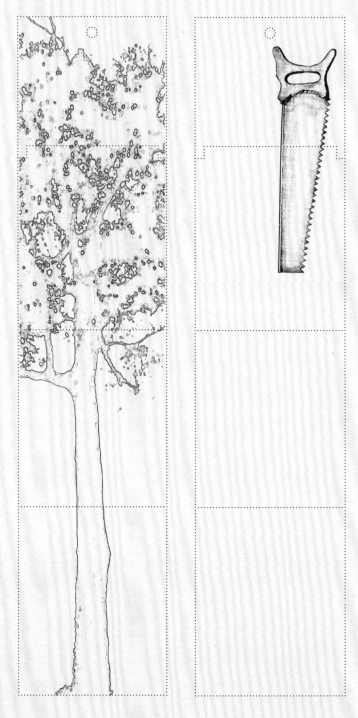

36

don't have enough room in your apartment to have the right number of seats for the number of guests you want to have. Typically the spartan, unsightly seat is hidden away somewhere, only to be pulled out when company arrives. And as soon as the guests leave your house you hide the chairs. You shove them under the bed, in your closet, wherever you have space for them, which is ironic. If I hide ugly spare seating in my closet, why do I use it for entertaining? Why do we invite guests to sit on a piece of furniture we're not proud of? What's more,

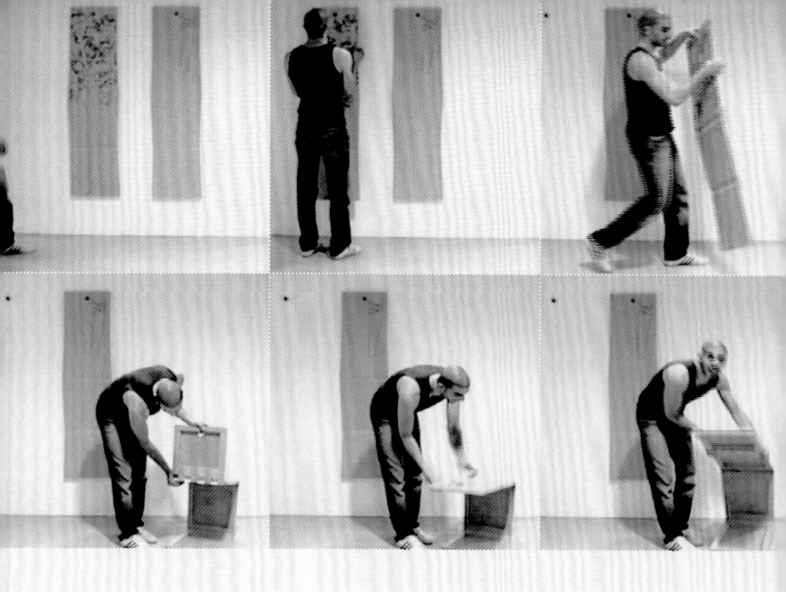

if we don't have room to accommodate extra seating, we probably don't have much storage space, either.

The opposite of an object you're not proud of is one that you're supremely delighted by, as with art. I thought, Let the guests sit on a piece that hangs on the wall and that you can enjoy when guests are not there. My solution for improving the standard seat plays with this duality; I saw an opportunity to make a chair that functioned as both a work of art

and a place to sit. I wanted to start collaborating with artists and have them use the Pick Chair as a blank canvas, creating different interpretations and editions. And I knew that its physical transformation needed to be seamless—otherwise, the conversion would unfold in a mechanical step-by-step process and detract from the allure of change.

The Pick Chair is a canvas with movable joints, where its surfaces double as a place for art. Its hinged metal framework comprises four panels,

The very first Saw & Tree Pick Chairs
in production with Italian manufacturer BBB

with a small hole in the top one. The chair can therefore be hung on a wall when not in use, and morphs into a seat with a single gesture: simply set it upright on the ground and its hinges pivot to form a sturdy base, seat, and back. What's striking about the Pick Chair is its smooth transition from the 3D (an object) to 2D (an artwork). It stands at the intersection of these dimensions, and paved the way for the recurring theme of transformation in our studio's work today.

After the school prototypes, one of the things that I was playing with is the idea of cutting wood, cutting a tree, making a piece of furniture and then stitching it back to being a tree again. So that was the very first graphic that I created for the Pick Chair.

Later on, when the publisher Mondadori was celebrating its 100-year anniversary they asked us to do an edition. So I took one of my favorite books, Shel Silverstein's *The Giving Tree,* as inspi-

ration and applied text from the book to the chairs, symbolizing the cycle of a tree.

Some years later, *Clear Magazine* asked me if I could make clear chairs for them. They proposed an event at the top of the Rockefeller Center and they had no budget to make the chairs. I remember taking a ride somewhere and meeting with Michael Shvo, a prominent New York real estate broker and later developer. Some weeks earlier I had read an article about him in which he said, "I want to change the New York skyline."

Special edition for *Clear Magazine* with a new skyline for Manhattan

I saw an interesting opportunity to invite him to change the landscape of New York City on clear chairs hanging from the balcony at The Top of the Rock. He got very excited and sponsored the event, buying eighteen Pick Chairs. During the event I traced the landscape of New York in black and he added his vision of additional buildings between the skyscrapers. He still owns the collection. The most important thing that happened at this event was that I met my wife Davina, which forever changed the landscape of my life.

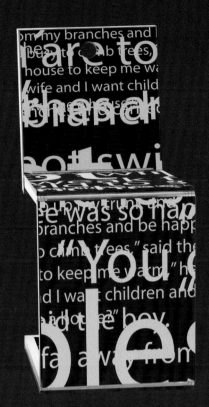

Special edition of 100 chairs for publishing house
Mondadori 's 100-year anniversary

The Pick Chair was in production with BBB for some years until they closed shop and we got the rights back. Recently we changed the design slightly, simplified the engineering so it could be made completely out of wood, and reduced the production cost.

Chapter 3

Urban Cast-Away

Can fur last forever?

For the second iteration of Construkt, Marithé + François Girbaud's quarterly series of artist-designed objects, the French clothier asked us to create limited-edition pieces that related to its aesthetic. As I considered the brand, the most compelling aspect was how it addressed controversial subjects through each collection—its clothing made a statement in more ways than one.

Vintage fur dipped in liquid porcelain solidifies into organic shapes in the kiln.

MFG was extremely experimental and political with his themes and when he asked us to create a jewelry collection without any particular brief, I was wondering why he would hire somebody like me, who is not trained as a jewelry designer, to create jewelry. This openness set the stage for our exploration and created a space for chance to play a role in the production of the pieces.

I wanted to make my own statement that related to both product design and fashion. Jewelry presented a

fitting liaison between the two worlds, as the typology often crosses over from one to the other. I decided to use fur as my politically charged component, and porcelain as a reference to product. At that time I was fascinated with porcelain. Porcelain represents, for me, a very high-end material to use in a product application. The protests against fur couture seemed at their height at that time so I was interested in making a statement by using fur and giving it a different meaning, a different life. The elements were in many ways in opposition to one another: one is natural and tactile; the other is harsh and solid.

So we were experimenting in the shop dipping vintage fur into liquid porcelain. Each night we would fire the pieces and see the results the next day, and we were fascinated everyday by the results. Some did not look as magical but some were like seeing shapes in clouds, with forms that resembled birds or movements of water. We didn't have intention or control: as the fur burned away the porcelain solidified the form. So it was a very organic process guided by the medium.

It became a collection of eighteen one-of-a-kind pieces. Today some of the collection is in the permanent collection of the Museum of Arts and Design, and others are with jewelry collectors around the world.

....

Some were like seeing shapes in clouds, the forms resembled birds or movements of water.

Chapter 4

Skins

One bone, multiple skins.

Skins is one of our projects where the client had a basis of the concept. We developed this concept after the owner of the company reached out to us with the 'skin and bones' approach in mind and asked if we would design the collection of shoes as well as the packaging and branding. In early 2007, Skins debuted with an entirely new footwear concept. An amalgamation of luxury, technology,

and design, it was an innovative two-part, mix-and-match footwear concept consisting of outer collapsible "skins" (the shell and sole) and a highly engineered flexible form, the "bone," that cradles the foot. Our studio contributed to the overall design of Skins' brand identity, packaging, and display, as well as the styling of the inner bone form.

We found it compelling because we could relate to the idea of separating two things that exist within one product. A shoe has functional purpose

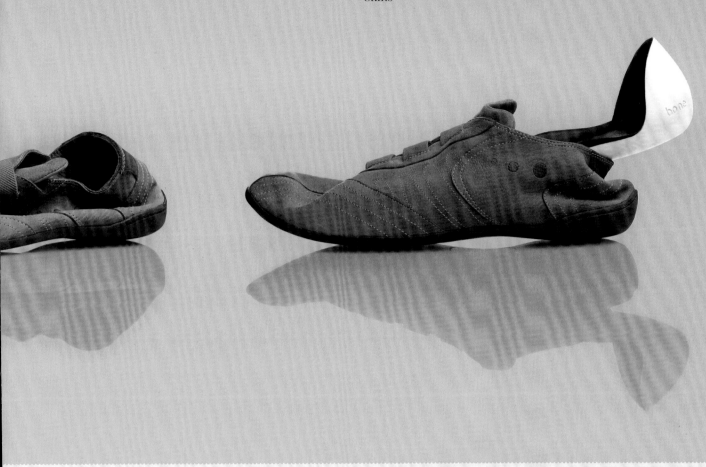

and needs to be orthopedic, and at the same time it needs to look good. Fashion changes but the comfort remains the same. In essence, you start with one bone and then you can choose from a lot of different skins that you interchange.

So we created two very different packaging styles, a logo and a campaign around the skin and the bone concept, and the idea of the natural body, being naked, along with the concept of interchangeability, of being dressed in different ways.

The product enjoyed a limited launch, and it was a very interesting undertaking for us. It introduced us to the model of a service that crossed the boundaries from product design to art direction, packaging, graphic design, and branding. It was really the first time that we created a holistic design package for a client.

Chapter 5

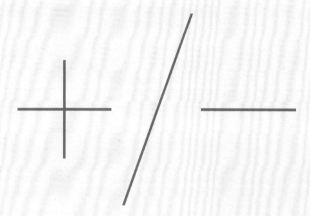

One simple gesture replaces a series of actions.

Boffi challenged us to think about innovation in the bathroom. I was already absolutely amazed with Boffi's aesthetic, quality, and attention to detail. Only a couple of companies today reach that kind of standard. Their challenge to us: "There's not a lot of innovation in the bathroom today; how can you improve the bathroom environment?"

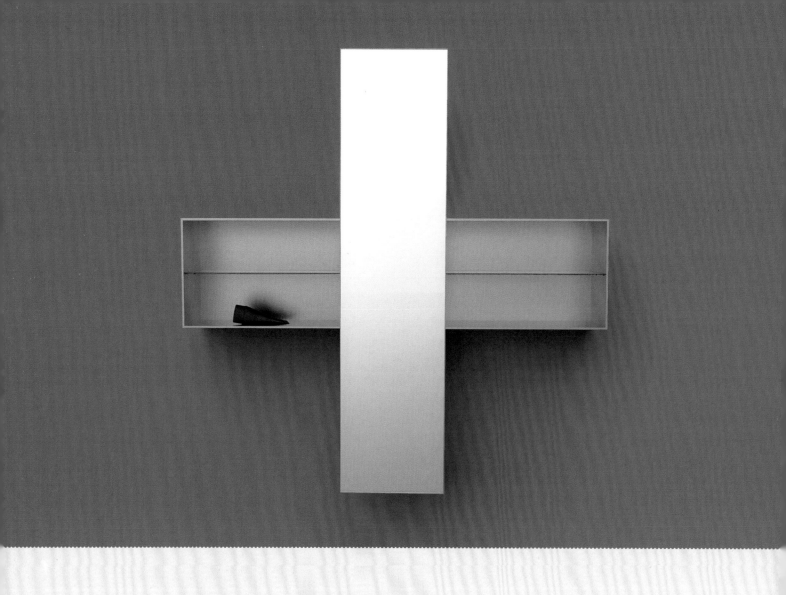

I started thinking about my medicine cabinet—a lavatory essential that's a constant focal point during my morning routine. I'll open the door to get something from inside then close it to use the mirror, only to open and close the door again to put the toiletry away. People can do this dozens of times while getting ready. Could this repetitive, disruptive action be replaced with a single gesture? I realized the movement that would achieve this functionality was a simple rotation. So the idea of the "plus/minus" was born: swinging open and closed around a center pin, a pivot point.

The +/- cabinet consists of a horizontal storage space that minimizes mess. To open, rotate the mirrored door 90 degrees, forming a cross-shaped cabinet that reveals a shelved interior, allowing uninterrupted access to the objects inside. In the vertical position the mirror focuses on the user and allows access to either side of the cabinet.

Under the same banner of innovation, I created a second cabinet with a different motivation: In compact urban residences, counter space is scarce —especially in bathrooms, where there's rarely a non-water-soaked space to place toiletries. My solution was Dry, a medicine cabinet marked by its glass double doors that open vertically from the center. The bottom door falls open into a deep ledge, providing a place to put objects while interacting with the sink. The top door, which covers part of the cabinet's shelved interior, hides objects that are only used seasonally or in emergency, leaving space below for toiletries used every day.

+/- won the Good Design award in 2008.

Chapter 6

Davina

Expressing the signature finish with a single fold.

Italian door manufacturer Lualdi debuted its first collection designed by US-based architects in 2010. Lualdi is known for their products' minimal aesthetic and high-end finishes. I think the reason for their succes is their drive for perfect manufacturing, down to the hinges and closures...and that they go the extra mile with a lacquer like that on Ferrari cars,

which are dipped seven times and
have a very distinct finish. That was
our starting point in thinking of how
to create a new door for Lualdi. Our
contribution to the collection is a door
affectionately named Davina.

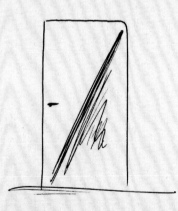

When we represent something that has a high-
gloss finish in a graphic form we always do it with
a 45-degree line that represents the reflective
shine. So the idea was to have a door with a crease

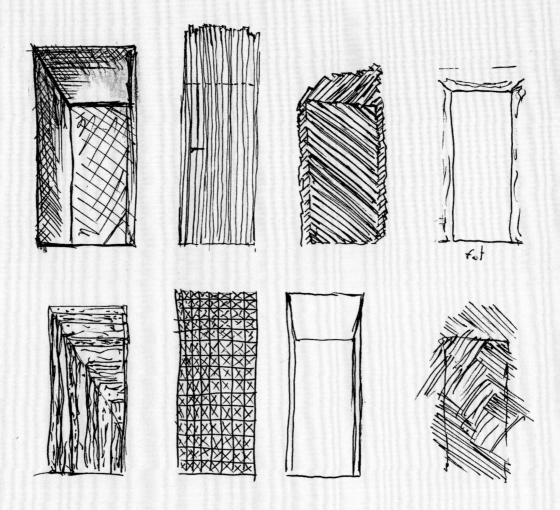

running diagonally from corner to corner and it also actually creates a little opening at the edges, an inviting subtlety. A simple diagonal fold creates a two-toned depth that subtly reveals the inside door frame, creating the illusion that it is slightly ajar. There are different hinge connections at the top and bottom so when the door is open it looks as if it's slanted but it's only partially slanted in reality and that effect happens on both sides of the door. The Davina door was produced in red, black, and white.

....

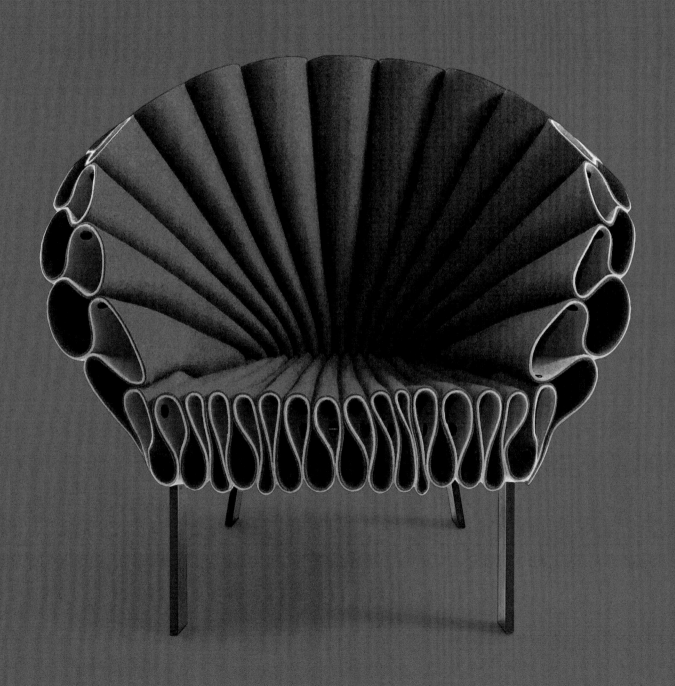

Chapter 7

Peacock Chair

How can a single sheet of fabric create structure?

This project started with a very personal story. What year was it? I think it was 2009. At the time, I was splitting up with a girlfriend and was trying to process my heartbreak. It was hard, but I love the strength that comes from vulnerability, and the uniqueness of the scars and impressions that life events leave behind.

Three sheets of fabric fold into shape with no glue, sewing or traditional upholstery techniques.

I thought to myself, "Well, should I build a wall or should I be naked?" And those two extreme approaches—should I completely disconnect or should I just embrace it—really brought me back to think of dance again. I've always found that the analogies of body movement have a lot of influence on the way I think.

And I thought about how dance is like an alternation of falling forward and falling backward, and how very performative animals, like the peacock, display this duality of form. The peacock opens up its feathers for two conflicting reasons. One is attraction and the other is defense—which is exactly the opposite. One is to say, "Look at how big and beautiful I am" and the other is to say, "Stay away. I'm a bigger animal than you think I am."

This analogy helped me to look at the forms and look at ways to create structure from something that has no structural integrity. The material felt is essentially pressed wool. As opposed to woven fabric, it receives its structural integrity from compression—simply from pressure. So we looked at how we could create pressure from folds and strength from folds.

The Peacock Chair is a simple metal ring and four legs that allow for three sheets of felt woven on to them. The chair uses no traditional upholstery techniques— no glue, no stitching. It's just the pressure of the felt on the metal and the rivets that keep the edges together.

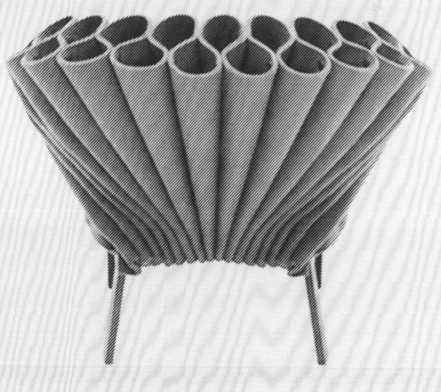

We showed the idea to Cappellini and they added the Peacock Chair to their collection. The chair became one of our best known and iconic pieces for the studio. It's been on many magazine covers and included in other publications. Later on, we were surprised to see that it was featured in Rihanna's "S&M" video. Ironically, the video premiered the same week that the Peacock Chair was accepted into the permanent collection of the Metropolitan Museum of Art.

This sparked a discussion in the studio about what is more important: being in one of the most important museums in the world or being featured in a video that received more than 40 million views in one week. And we didn't really come up with a conclusion. Or the conclusion was that both of them are important in different ways—for the world of pop culture and the world of culture in general. And I think that when we are then talking again about the value in approaching things in different ways at one time, something may mean one thing in one industry and something completely different in another. I think that the value and improvement in well-being that comes when approaching a project from different worlds is quite promising.

Chapter 8

Bentley

Can a car body share the same emotion as the active living transformative driving experience?

We were invited to think about an idea for Bentley Motors. It wasn't really a concept car commission but really more of a conceptual commission themed around this question: How should we be thinking about cars in the future? One of the things that I found really fascinating is the relationship

of the human body to the body of a car. If we look at the car quite literally as an extension of our body and consider how our body adjusts to different situations—how our skin reflects the muscular changes that happen within our body, for example—the car body doesn't share any of that experience. It doesn't change its appearance whether it's driving slow or fast, in one set of conditions or another, with people or alone, standing in traffic or on a highway.

So we collaborated with dancers and a choreographer from the prestigious Cedar Lake Ballet as well as videographer Erez Sabag, and created a video piece that explores an analogy between the human body and the car. We established sets of movements that the car body can adjust to based on the driving conditions. For instance, the front of the car becomes slightly sportier and more aerodynamic when the car drives faster. When it sits at a traffic light it stands proud, higher, and the front is more elevated. And then the back of the vehicle, very much like a horse that moves faster and expands its muscular structure, also widens and occupies more space when it drives faster. Why do I need door handles outside after I'm inside the car? Now in new cars we see this feature collapse. They completely disappear and go inside, so as not to interfere with the beautiful flow of the body.

The work that we did for Bentley ended up being an art installation, a video that we presented during Art Basel in 2007. It became promotional material for Bentley and we extracted from the video some very beautiful imagery which we keep as inspiration today.

....

The car as an extension of the human body.

Chapter 9

Tron Chair

When digital and physical collide.

The physics of collision has long intrigued us. We were fascinated by the challenge of translating the concept of collision from digital to physical and vice versa. We're constantly considering this; our digital shop and a physical workshop are not in the same space, and the results of each can yield very disparate results. We want to utilize as many avenues for inspiration as possible.

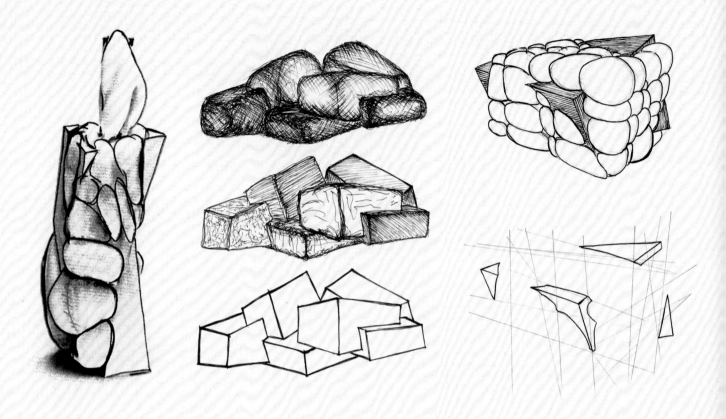

This experimentation occurs in both of our studio's spaces in different ways. Our curiosity grew when we considered how results differ when conducted in the digital realm; instead of producing a messy aftermath as with a physical impact, objects simply intersect with each other. If you think about two cars driving into each other, the collision is chaotic, parts are flying all over the place. How exactly they collide depends on many factors: angle, speed, strength of the

material and so forth. This type of car smashes this way—that car smashes that way. Trying to replicate that digitally is extremely complex. And that is often true when taking a process in the opposite direction as well. If you look at two forms colliding digitally and occupying the same space and try to manufacture that, replicating it physically is very challenging. To underscore this contrast, we wanted to make a silhouette that is informed by both physical and digital events.

One of the things that we wanted to look at was how to create a chair that was born in both worlds at the same time. If you look at the four sides that this chair has: arms, a backrest and a seat, there are basically eight forms. We began by creating four rectangular prisms on a computer and four similar shapes by hand. We then collided the handmade forms physically, 3D-scanned them, and digitally merged them with the digital forms. The irregular result provided the blueprint for our distinctive chair.

We were calling it the Calculated Collision Chair. When we showed it to Giulio Cappellini, he said, "I've just been approached by Disney to think about *TRON: Legacy*. This is exactly the story of the movie: the world of the digital colliding with the world of the physical. Why don't we create it for the film?"

The lounger was manufactured by Cappellini in collaboration with Disney. Its shape resembled the film's jagged, angular terrain, which was also built from digital and analog data. It was deemed the Tron Chair.

It wasn't included in the movie because filming was already underway and our production schedules didn't align, but it was featured at the debut of the film and lead actress Olivia Wilde traveled with it to the numerous premiere events.

Tron Chair

Giulio Cappellini

We presented a limited edition of the roto-molded plastic seats at Design Miami in 2010 and Salone del Mobile 2011. Cappellini continues to produce the chair in four matte colors: white, gray, blue, and green.

....

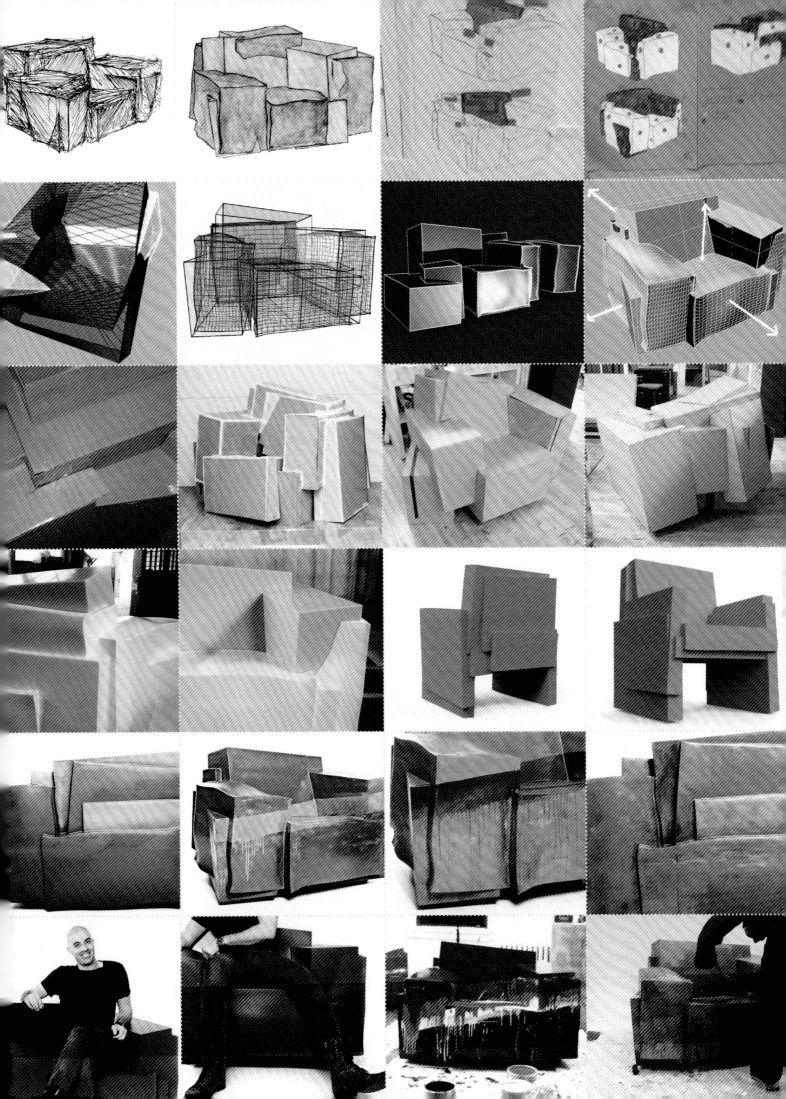

Chapter 10

Tumi

Can luggage transform to fit all your travel needs?

Our collection for Tumi—the world's leading travel accessory brand—was their first-ever collaboration with an external designer. When Tumi asked us to create a collection of luggage I was very excited for a couple of reasons. One, I was already a Tumi customer, and I think that working on projects where you think of yourself first as a customer can be very intuitive. Two, as a frequent traveler, the typical problems with luggage and the opportunities for improvement were familiar to me.

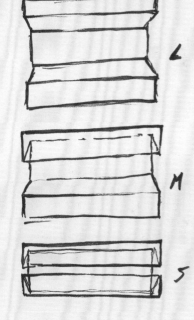

I had a strong desire to create a line that would improve the travel experience. As a frequent flyer, I identified with the multifaceted life of a contemporary traveler: depending on lots of factors—where I go, the time of year, how long I'll stay, and the purpose of the trip—the contents, size, and number of my bags varies. What's more, my needs could change within a single trip, requiring a small carry-on at departure but a large, checked bag upon return. How could a single piece of luggage accommodate every scenario on the go?

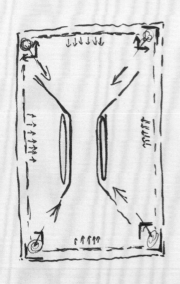

I thought that this angle was the best way to approach this project: not to start with any preordained aesthetic approaches but to look first at what can make the travel experience easier. What can make it more logical? When you start thinking about luggage and travel bags, you realize how attached to them you are, physically. You are literally holding your bag for hours and hours, and it becomes an extension of your body as well. This made us think that the bags had to be able to shift posture and profile depending on the conditions.

And the fact is that we constantly carry different contents to different places. We go to Costa Rica with flip-flops and two T-shirts; we go to Russia with a coat and five sweaters. We go to visit our families with a lot of gifts, we go to trade shows and come back with a lot of materials, we go to Italy and come back with new clothes, and so forth. The contents of our bags constantly change even if we don't travel far, even if we leave our apartment and want to go to the gym on the way to work or to an event after and then to the gym and then home; we carry different things

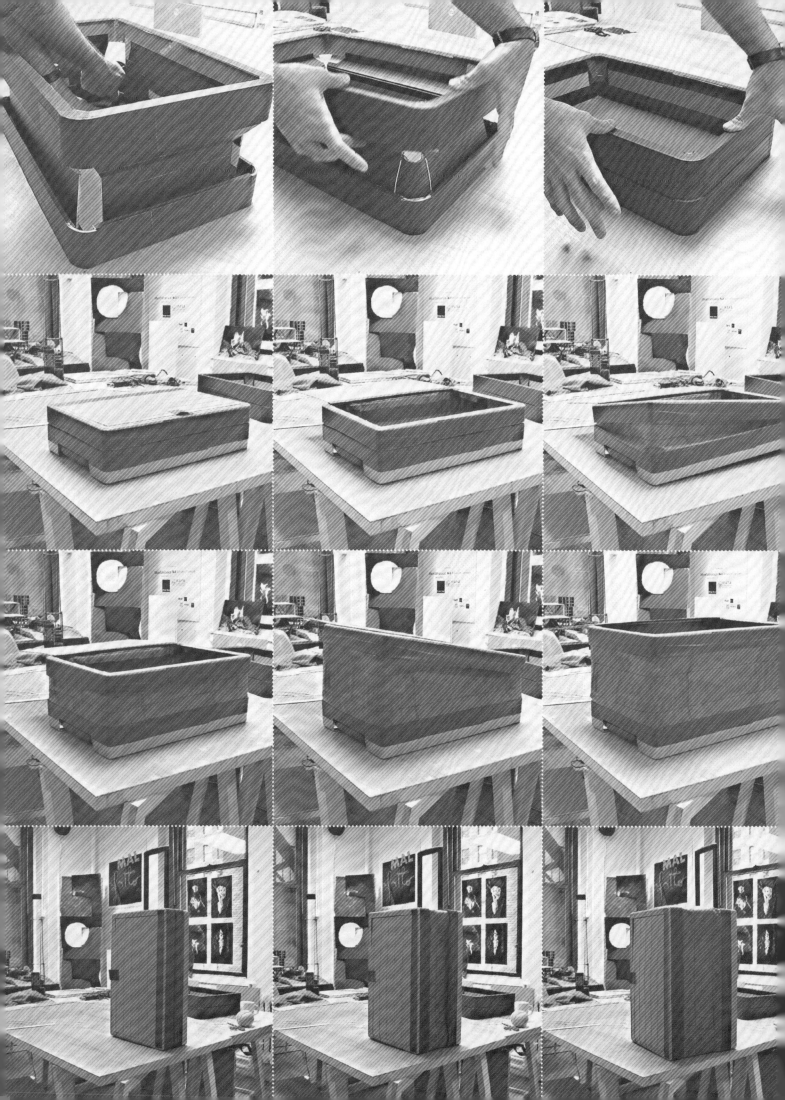

for different purposes. The idea of transformation was very much inherent in the desire to create a collection that can adapt on demand as quickly as possible to our ever-changing needs.

After eighteen months of research and prototyping, we developed an eleven-piece collection capable of dynamic transformation. The International Carry-On, the first-ever expandable zipperless hardcase, epitomizes this theme. It doubles in capacity through three different sizes—from 30 to 45 to 60 liters—

using a custom "living hinge": a unique two-stage transformation facilitated by two pairs of handles hidden inside. Squeeze and pull the innermost pair to reveal the first half of the expansion; an additional set of handles enables the maximum increase. So what we created was a suitcase that can be a small carry-on, a medium size carry-on, or a large bag that needs to be checked.

The big advantage of this bag and one of the most interesting things for me was how this ability to play

with the content and the size addressed the issues that I identified with my travel needs. I'd arrive at the airport and be thinking "I'm going to land at 2 AM, I'm going to be tired, all I want is to go home, what can I do so I don't need to check my luggage?" So, I'd take out the big coat, carry it with me and be able to collapse this bag so I can use it as a carry on. Or alternatively, I land and I don't care, I want to stow all my things so I can be free to walk around the duty free shop. So, we have the ability to change and to play and I think for customers of Tumi that's

a massive advantage, saving twenty minutes in the middle of the night coming back from the airport a few times a month...it's worth paying a couple of hundred dollars more on a suitcase. I think that's what made this bag the best-seller in the collection.

The bag's faceted surface derived from our attempt to make the hardcase lightweight by reducing its thickness. The logic of creating creases is seen in stainless steel sinks and A/C ducts: apply a pleat to a thin material, and the fold creates strength.

We made this beautiful geometry the signature of the collection, and adapted the triangular designs to the bag's front and back, as well as into leather, zipper pulls, handles, and more.

The backpack is a very important piece for me because for a long time I was never a backpack customer. I never thought about buying a backpack. But then I tested some of Tumi's backpacks and thought, "Wow, having two straps on your shoulders, and being able to hold an umbrella and a coffee

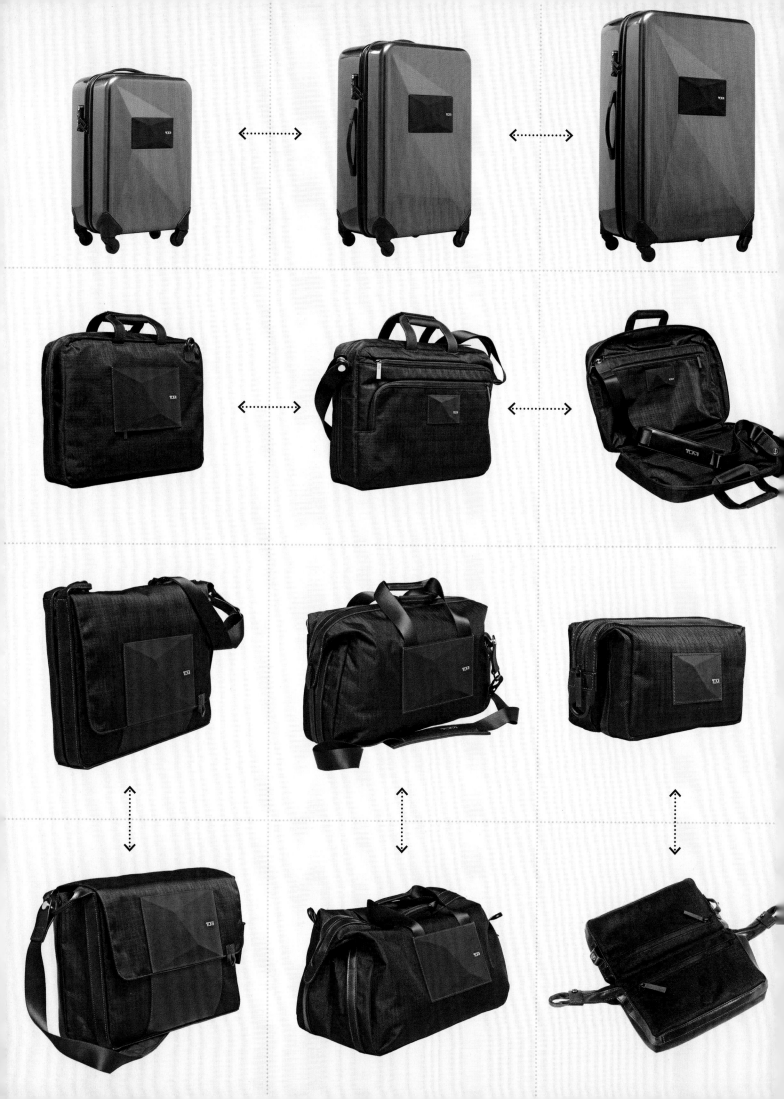

while walking around Milan the whole day would be great!" But, did I really want to walk into a meeting with a backpack? No. So how could I hide the straps and convert it into something that looks nothing like a backpack and looks more like a tote bag? That was really the impetus of this bag. We don't think about that until we have the option to have a backpack that you can convert into a tote bag in an elevator, and change it right back into a backpack.

I think that another change in the past few years is that we are carrying less and less paper, and computers are lighter and smaller now. But at the same time, we still have our sport shoes and other gear so really the ability to move from something that is extra-small to something extra-large was a big part of the motivation. Every piece in the collection has that capacity to transform from very small to very large.

Take the toiletries bag, for instance; we were thinking about this bag and realizing that it's always the last piece that you put in your luggage. Why? Because you want to brush your teeth before you go to the airport at 1 AM so you leave it out and of course you've ne-glected to allow room for it in your bag so you have to squeeze everything, and your shirts get wrinkled. But instead of looking at it as a block, we considered how to open it up and lay it flat, because you always have

at least an inch of room on top. Based on that logic and form, it also made sense that we take advantage of the separation of the two sides in order to have wet items on one side and dry items on the other. A big advantage of this configuration is that the back-side is pretty nondescript and has additional zippers, as we often travel with a passport or cash or things we don't want people to find.

So truly, everything in the collection approaches the concept of transformation to accommodate

different needs and lifestyles. We pushed the boundaries of engineering and manufacturing and every component, from wheels to frame, needed to be custom-molded for this collection. The resulting objects invite users to spontaneously customize their luggage as a transformable extension of their lives.

They asked us to look at how the collection should be presented and communicated. We created videos and all the collateral materials around the collection. When it debuted, the inventory that Tumi

had forecasted for an entire year sold in two months, so it was incredibly successful commercially and one of the most rewarding things for us was that our engagement with Tumi continued into other areas of their business, from product design into retail design and creative direction.

Retail

Later we started working on the Tumi stores, which themselves constitute a very interesting story. It's another example that highlights this holistic nature of design. Typically retail design doesn't take into account elements that aren't part of the physical environment: what music are they going to play in the store? What is the logic and the operation of merchandizing? What outfits are the sales people going to wear? And those are the things that most interest us because they are fundamental to the experience of shopping at a retail store.

When Tumi engaged us this time, it had just gone public, so they could share a lot of data with us that they weren't able to before. One of the things they shared with us is how many units each of their products sells. We converted that data into an infographic in which the quantity of sales determined the size of the graphic representing an item. Because they had hundreds of products for sale, the chart went on for so long that the lowest-selling products were so small they weren't even recognizable on the page. We said, "Tumi, you are asking us to take all your items out, make a beautiful story, and put all the items back. But look at your products on this chart, these successful ones here are the same size as those in real life, but over on this page they're reproduced as minuscule, based on their sales." We suspected there were too many SKUs. So we suggested, "What if instead of having five items on each shelf we have four items on each

Rolling bags on the floor

Handheld luggage on the wall

Accessories on the table

shelf? Can we run a test and see how the stores perform?" We encouraged Tumi to do a test where for a period of time they eliminated 20 percent of their least popular products. Because we really believe in the paradox of choice: that the more options you have, the harder it is to decide and the more likely you are to be unhappy with your choice. They came back after a month of running the test in three stores, and said "Dror, these three stores, on average, sold 60 percent more than what they normally sell with 20 percent less

product." So then we were thinking, "Well, then you can merchandize 20 percent less, manufacture 20 percent less, ship 20 percent less, handle 20 percent less, sell 60 percent more, and we haven't even started designing the store yet!" So this was one of the biggest contributions to Tumi as part of the process, even before design was underway.

The second big revelation was that Tumi used to merchandize by collection and we revolutionized their layout. The Dror collection would have stood in one place and other collections would stand together separately. When we went to the stores and observed how people shopped we realized that most customers that entered the store actually knew exactly what they were looking for.

And if for example they were looking for a document bag, the sales person would go around the store picking up different bags from different collections, put them in front of the customer and say, "This one is $120, this is $140, this is $160, these are the materials..." and then whether the customer bought one or not they would have to go back and return all the items to their various locations. So we asked why the store wasn't organized to facilitate that pattern.

In considering the layout, we thought about how to display merchandise divided by the three types of display areas: floors, walls, and tables. We imposed a very simple logic. Bags, which you carry with your hands, are all on shelves because you want them to be at your level. If you buy a suitcase you don't wave it in the air to show your friends. So the suitcases are on the floor, the bags are on the wall, and all the accessories are placed on tables, just like candy stores, just like bookstores. When you enter the store, its logic is presented right away: men's, women's, bags, suitcases, accessories.

Another consideration we shared with them was: When do people buy bags most? Tumi is popular with business people, professionals, and world travelers. We realized that people buy bags primarily when they are getting a promotion or going on holiday. Why? Because you don't want to travel with your old crappy luggage, or you upgraded to a corner office and you want to walk in with a new bag. We thought about the excitement before those events. You come home and you tell your partner "I got promoted!" What kind of music would be playing in the background? We were thinking that music should be playing in the store. It's not Amy Winehouse's "Back to Black." It's exciting, it's *Ocean's Eleven*, "I-hit-the-jackpot" music. So they changed the playlist to reflect that mood as well.

When they re-opened the flagship store, the sales expectations were not too high because they had two other stores close by, competing for sales. Despite this, it became Tumi's bestselling store worldwide per square foot. After the success of the flagship, they enrolled stores in our design approach worldwide.

We are constantly talking about Tumi because they engaged almost all of our disciplines—product design to interior design to art direction and more—and also because of their focus on innovation and excellence, which resonates with what we aim to do everyday.

....

Chapter 11
Yigal Azrouël

How to translate the essence of a design from one discipline to another?

Fashion designer Yigal Azrouël—my uncle (and one my best friends)—was working to open his first retail location in 2002, and I was very interested in the design challenge. Yigal said to me, "But you're not an interior designer, so how would you do it?" I had to explain that although I hadn't trained as an interior designer, I still wanted do this project. Even though

I was competing with others who were interior designers, he liked the approach we submitted and it became the studio's first full interior design project.

I think it's very interesting to dive into territories that you're not comfortable in, working with specialists that can assist you to achieve a vision. Years later, we're still in the same position, we're still being asked about our expertise and specialties, still today being doubted by potential clients who usually hire specialists to do projects for them. It's wonderful when clients understand this approach as a strength of ours. Although I have, at times, wished that we would never again have to say, "This is the first time we're doing this," now I can tell you that I hope to be saying that for the rest of my career.

The Yigal Azrouël store got a lot of recognition and press for being one of the first high-end stores in New York City's Meatpacking District. The place had so much character when we found it; it had actually been a meat locker, and some of the mechanical

elements were penetrating through the walls, through the beams and bricks. I found it very seductive, very sexual. I thought it would make sense to use that as a motive for a fashion designer that is talking about similar attributes of sensuality, sexuality.

At the time, Yigal was extremely experimental with his work, so the store needed to reflect that. For instance, the beams were covered with powdered iron so they rusted over time. Everything new that we incorporated into the existing space moved and penetrated through environments.

The store was unconventional at the time in that we designed it to be quite dark, with the attention to the product defined by single, stark light sources. It was extremely theatrical.

Later as we worked on more of Yigal's stores, this first project became a reference point for us in terms of process. At that time I was pretty much working on the store from inside the space, sketching designs, working with the contractors, carving pieces of stone, and it was an incredible schooling. We documented the entire process and still work in that immersive style today.

....

Chapter 12

Soho Synagogue

Reinventing tradition in the heart of the city.

The Soho Synagogue is, surprisingly, the New York neighborhood's first synagogue and represents a fresh vision that translates the inspiration of Judaism for a new generation. The temple was designed to be a sanctuary for the community. I met with Rabbi Dovi Scheiner; when he told me where he was going to put the synagogue I thought it was absolutely crazy.

He wanted to take a former Gucci store and turn it into a synagogue. I wondered, "How are you going to afford rent? How are you going to be able to stay in the community in Soho?" But he did it, he put it together and found the funds and created something extremely powerful. I think for me this project represents an interesting case: we often feel that we are trying to push our clients further and stretch them out of their comfort zones, and in this particular case it was the client who was stretching us and pushing us even further. He'd say, "I don't care. I want to see if we can do something much more radical." So we started with the appearance. Usually synagogues or churches are not retail stores and don't have that kind of storefront presence, but in New York City, why not?

We took as a given the mindset of lower Manhattan's Jewish community was fairly open, so our design sought to create a space in which the traditions and fundamental functions of the synagogue can be practiced within a contemporary, informal setting.

The main focus in a synagogue is the ark, *aron* in Hebrew, which is usually where the Torah is held and what the congregation faces. It is typically a rectangular wooden case. But instead, we were looking at the idea of a circle as the focal point of attention; and dividing it into three. I was thinking this could echo the effect of how projected light breaks down into red, green, and blue (RGB), with three circles coming

together to form one bright, white light. We came up with the idea of two circles coming together to enclose the scripture inside. It's a ritual that rabbis have always done in a synagogue, opening and closing the doors as part of the experience of worship. So the placement of two triangles within the circular doors allows them to slide together to form the Star of David.

We created a space with a sense of privacy inside but that is also welcoming and not completely closed off to the neighborhood. We applied white lines to the exterior glass to reflect the striped symbols that exist in many Jewish traditions. This approach created an intentional effect at night: when the synagogue was lit from the interior the lines were inverted, and a reflection of glowing shadows appeared on the ground outside. Adding to the modern approach, a simple neon sign on the facade says SYNAGOGUE without any additional information. It is at once mysterious and inviting.

The interior space is equipped with a couple of different transformative elements that serve the needs of the community. The space easily changes configuration to accommodate sitting or standing, from dining to screening and other types of communal activities. We tried to play with dual meaning and the juxtaposition of time, culture, and place in the overall artistic direction and design.

SANCTUARY

Chapter 13

WeWork

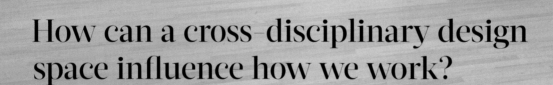

How can a cross-disciplinary design space influence how we work?

When we realized that we liked to experiment with radical approaches and concepts we thought, "Why don't we experiment with our own studio structure?" At that time our practice was on 39th Street in New York, in a nice private studio that took up half a floor and we wondered, "Imagine if all of the people that we collaborate with on a regular basis actually shared the floor with us?"

Adam Neumann had just founded WeWork's co-working community for small businesses, and said to me, "People with similar interests want to sit close to each other, so we're starting to think of organizing WeWork by disciplines. Would you be interested in coming and starting a floor of design and architecture?" I said, "Absolutely yes." If we can bring people whose work we admire, whose skills are complementary to the things that we're doing—together we could all collaborate and it could create an abundant atmosphere for ideas.

The idea for WeCross was to create a dynamic platform situated within WeWork's Soho West location. We moved our studio and brought together innovators and creative talents in disciplines that relate to design, architecture, interior design, graphic design, new technologies, communication, and more. For years we curated talented and strategic members to anchor a creative incubator that could collaboratively address design challenges, pool resources, lead research programs, and bring radical solutions. Focus groups could form on a project basis to conduct cross-disciplinary and unorthodox research with an immersive approach that reflects our global environment and contemporary culture.

To this day we value our community of collaborators and co-conspirators. Surrounding ourselves with people who inspire and push us forward helps to expand ourselves and find new possibilities in our lives.

....

Chapter 14

Eco
House

Can a house adapt to each season like we adapt our wardrobe?

As a practice we started out by coming up with ideas that no one had asked us to explore. All of them had something to do with transformation; all of them had a change of structure of some sort for different reasons, for different climates, needs, typologies.

In 2007 design critic and curator Aric Chen came for a studio visit and afterward he said, "Dror, your

work is very architectural." I went home really thinking about that and wondering what it meant. What about it is architectural? Does it mean my work is architectural because I like playing with structures? So the next day I came to the studio and I stared at my sketchbook and I drew an A-frame house and I started thinking, "Why does every kid around the world draw a house like that? I started opening some browsers and looking up A-frames, the origins of A-frames, the significance of A-frames, and the strength of a pitched roof. I

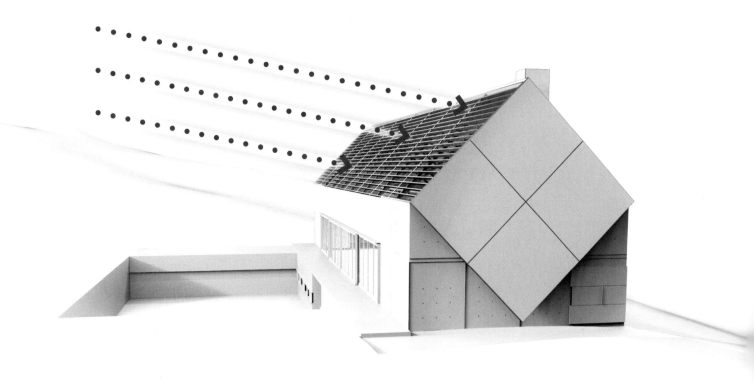

realized that triangulation is beneficial, it's great for load bearing, and it's easy to build. But then I was wondering, "Does every kid around the world draw an A-frame, even in places where they don't have pitched roofs like that?" And that made me think about where I live (in the northeast United States). We have four full seasons, a very warm summer and a very cold winter; we actually need the pitched roof. The primary purpose of pitching a roof is to redirect water and conserve heat. Thus, pitch is typically greater in areas of high rain or snowfall.

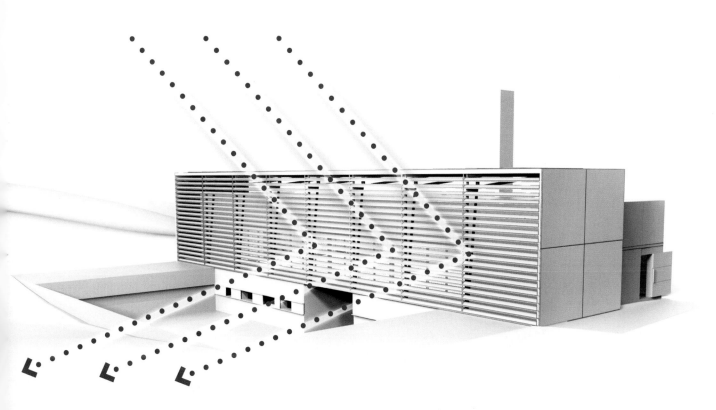

The idea for Eco House came from that interest in the different shapes and designs of roofs throughout time and cultures. I started with two Post-it notes on top of each other. Taking the two squares, I started hinging them and thinking, "What if we use hydraulic pistons to articulate a roof that goes up and down from being a 45-degree pitched roof to a flat roof? What could the benefits be? Can I have an indoor area in the winter that becomes outdoor in the summer? Can I get different benefits from the roof being down or up?"

So the Eco House is programmed to transform and adapt to the weather. We oriented the house so that during the winter it could take advantage of the sun and warm the house and so that during the summer it blocks the sun, creating shade and passive cooling mechanisms. When opened, the pitched roof allows for energy saving and channels rain water off. It becomes a second skin for the building distanced from the actual wall; it keeps the house cool and creates a ventilation system, while its solar panels also reflect the sunlight onto the pool to keep the water warm. A modular roof design transforms according to the season, responding to the natural environment. It's ideal for a continental climate such as that of the state of New York.

I was happy because it was our very first idea in architecture and because everybody in the studio at that time was part of this project. Everybody contributed to this idea and to the first conceptual presentation and that was very much the beginning of our architectural portfolio.

At this time we had just met the developer Michael Shvo, and he was very excited about our approach. Michael asked us: "Do you think you can handle a seven-story house?" I said, "Yes, we can. With support of specialists like we've done in other areas." He said, "I'm going to get you your first

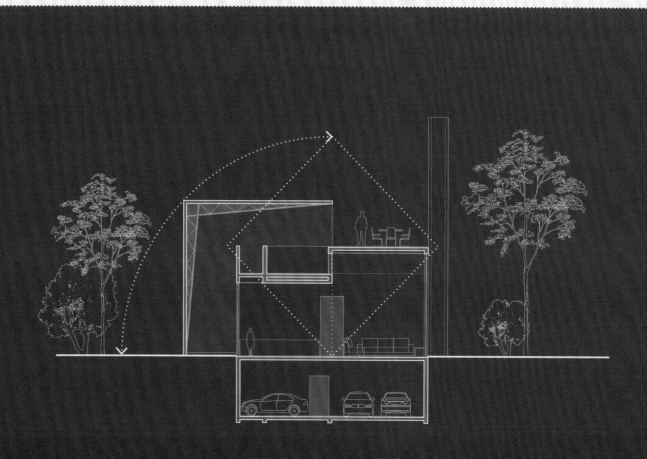

architectural project, give me three months." He actually kept his promise, called us two and a half months later and said "I have a project for you, but it's not seven stories, it's twenty-five. I'm going to introduce you to the developer behind the project and we're going to put you together with an architectural firm that will help you realize it and create an intelligent vision that is logical for the site."

And so we engaged on our first architectural commission. We demolished two existing town houses and broke ground, poured foundation, finished Construction Documents—and then the project stopped. The recession of 2008 hit, and the project, like so many, was put on hold; eventually the site was sold. But the development was extremely successful and it was well received by the client, the developer, and Michael Shvo. After this, Michael introduced us to another client, sparking what would become our second architectural commission, our first international commission, and our very first built project: Nurai (Chapter 21).

Chapter 15
Towers in the City

Cities today are more and more densely populated concrete jungles. Renovation and rebuilding are part of the cycle when a rare plot of land opens up. Once, when an empty lot appeared in downtown Manhattan, we wondered what kind of structure could grow there that would both enhance and respect its surroundings, complimenting and fostering healthy, historic elements of the urban fabric. That led us to consider how to apply new ideas to the other main issues around tall buildings in the city—context, opening up new views, and theatricality.

We designed three buildings that addressed and played with these ideas in different ways, exploring and creating new typologies for urban towers.

350 Bowery

350 Bowery consists of three curiously stacked glass volumes, each thoughtfully sized to align with its neighbors: the bases of the top and middle units follow horizontal planes formed by the roofs of adjacent buildings, kissing each structure's northeast edge in a gesture of respect. A forest of columns elevates the residential units to achieve this connection, creating an outdoor sculpture garden that offers glimpses of the surrounding environment.

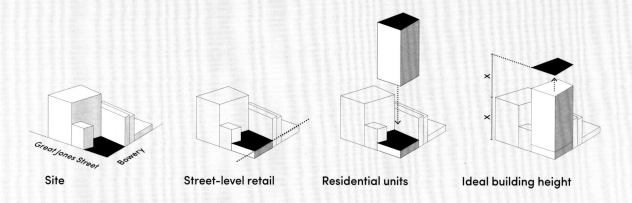

Site   Street-level retail   Residential units   Ideal building height

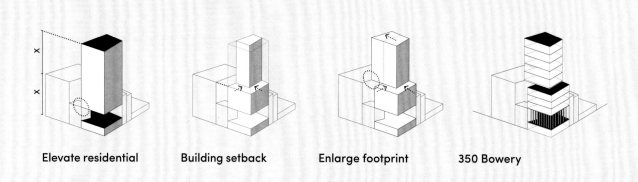

Elevate residential   Building setback   Enlarge footprint   350 Bowery

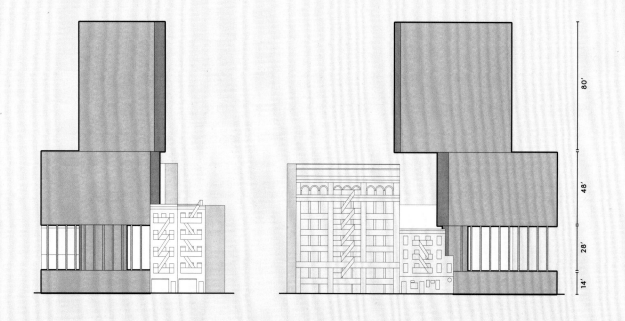

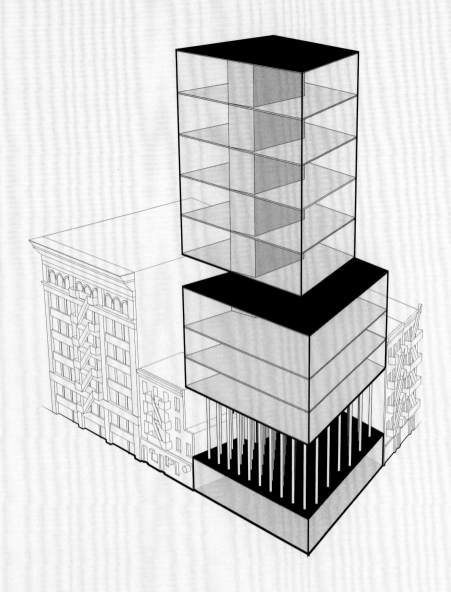

Anchored by a retail space at street level, 350 Bowery is a new typology of building that works with the existing local context to determine its distinctive shape. It looks at a couple of things: zoning limitations and how to interact with its neighbors. Now the building, instead of being shoulder to shoulder with the others, metaphorically kisses the buildings next to it and lifts residential units higher, creating more public space underneath, both indoors and outdoors.

281 Fifth Avenue

In a typical residential tower where floors are divided into four units, views from no more than two sides of the building are possible at a time. I started thinking about ways to incorporate a third view, supplying every tenant with the luxury of a vast, uninterrupted perspective.

Our concept for 281 Fifth Avenue achieves this feat by orienting its core structure into the shape of a pinwheel. A residence protrudes from each of the pinwheel's four arms on every floor, centralizing the unit's wet wall and support system on a single side. At the building's base, each arm fans out into a subtly curved V-shaped foot to form a strong, sculptural anchor. The pinwheel shape yields panoramic views to each unit.

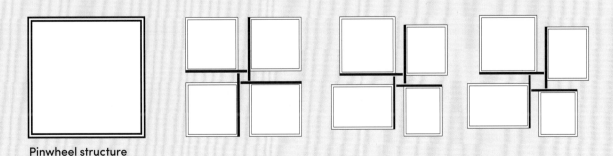

Pinwheel structure

In addition to providing each resident three completely glazed walls, this unique orientation lends itself to another indulgence: the opaque wall doubles as a projector screen. Real-time imagery of the environment directly behind the wall, captured by a camera attached to the adjacent unit, can be projected there, seamlessly connecting with existing views to provide a panoramic effect. The wall can also be used as a surface to view other media, or switched off completely.

In consideration of this particular site's zoning restrictions, part of the design motivation became elevating the building and starting the first floors much higher than a typical residential skyscraper. The base of the building reveals the structural logic of the pinwheel layout.

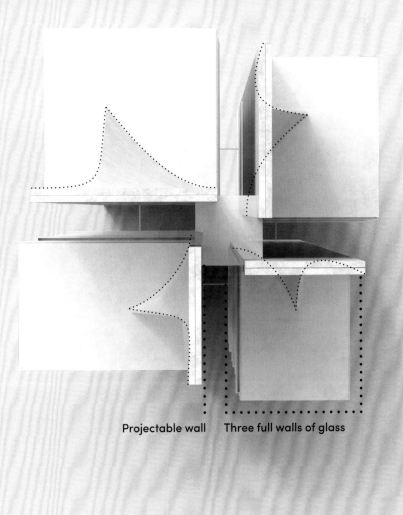

Projectable wall   Three full walls of glass

125 Greenwich

Michael Shvo had just purchased the site at 125 Greenwich Street and showed me a rendering of the proposed building, "a very skinny residential tower." Architect Rafael Viñoly had been commissioned to design the soaring, slender structure, which at the time was planned to be among the tallest residential buildings in New York City.

The first thing we asked when he showed us it was "What are those notches?" We found out that because the building is so tall, it needed to have three mechanical floors separating the sections. They are centralized spaces for climate controls, electrical panels, and other systems that are traditionally camouflaged by a building's facade. So we looked at it and considered that, as designers and as residents, we don't really care about or value mechanical floors like we do residential floors.

Instead of hiding mechanical floors in plain sight, why not make them galleries in the sky?

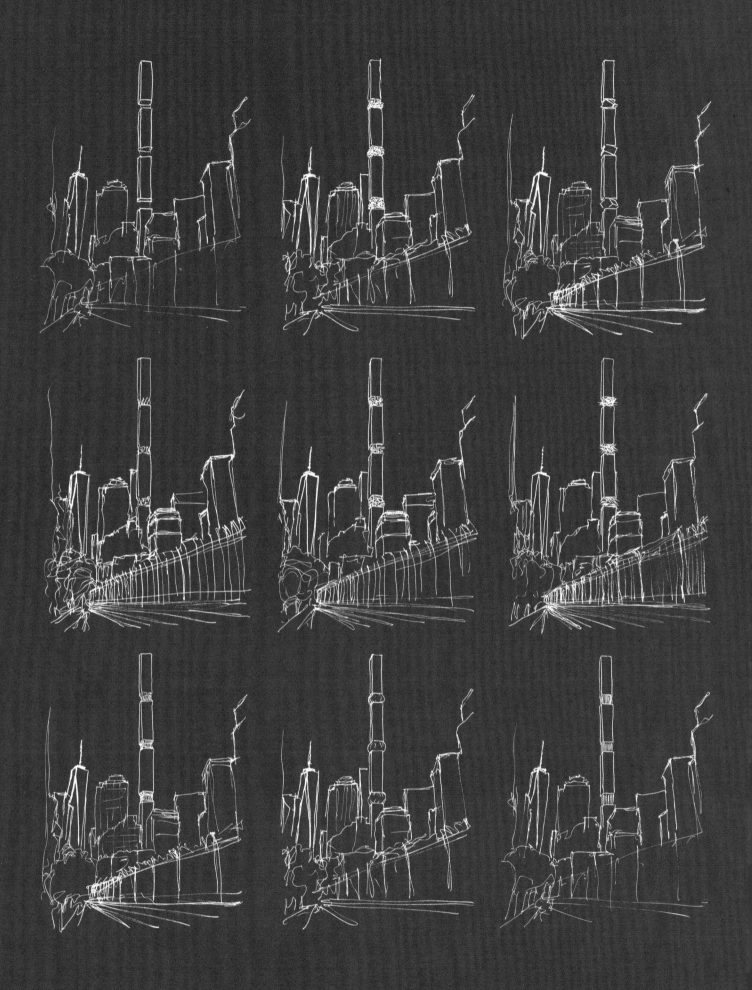

Mechanical floors are purely utilitarian and don't utilize the views, so we thought, Instead of hiding them in plain sight, why not bring these pockets of space to life? What if we look at it as residential floors that allow views out and mechanical floors that would let people look in? What if those spaces had another function as artwork? What if people seeing it in the city could enjoy it as a new experience?

And, of course, because it's supposed to be one of the tallest skyscrapers in New York you can see it from a lot of different places in the city. Situated within a building of such staggering height, the initiative could be the most-viewed public art project in the world.

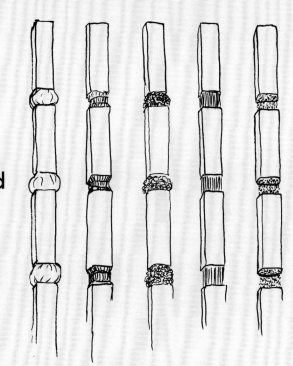

We conceived of the intervals as vitrines, an opportunity to showcase art: a highly visible, one-of-a-kind gallery in the sky. Our concept imagines each thirty-foot-tall mechanical bay as an exhibition space, where a different contemporary artist will display a site-specific installation each year. Through this intervention, we distinguish a major facet of the Manhattan skyline by transforming it into a beacon of contemporary creativity.

To initiate the project, we wanted the studio to be the first artists presenting an installation, so we started thinking about what we would do with the space. We decided to make it look as if there is nothing in those spaces at all. Our imagined artwork conveys the illusion of a building cut into four sections that "float" in mid-air. Created by state-of-the-art digital cameras and screens, the uncanny voids embrace the power of nothingness—it's a quiet gesture that I think has an irresistibly enchanting effect. Each screen projects images of the environment directly behind it, suggesting that one is looking through the building instead of at its facade.

Illustrating the potential for the concept to change the skyline of New York indefinitely, we envisioned a calendar of artist exhibitions for the first ten-year period.

2018

2022

2023

2024

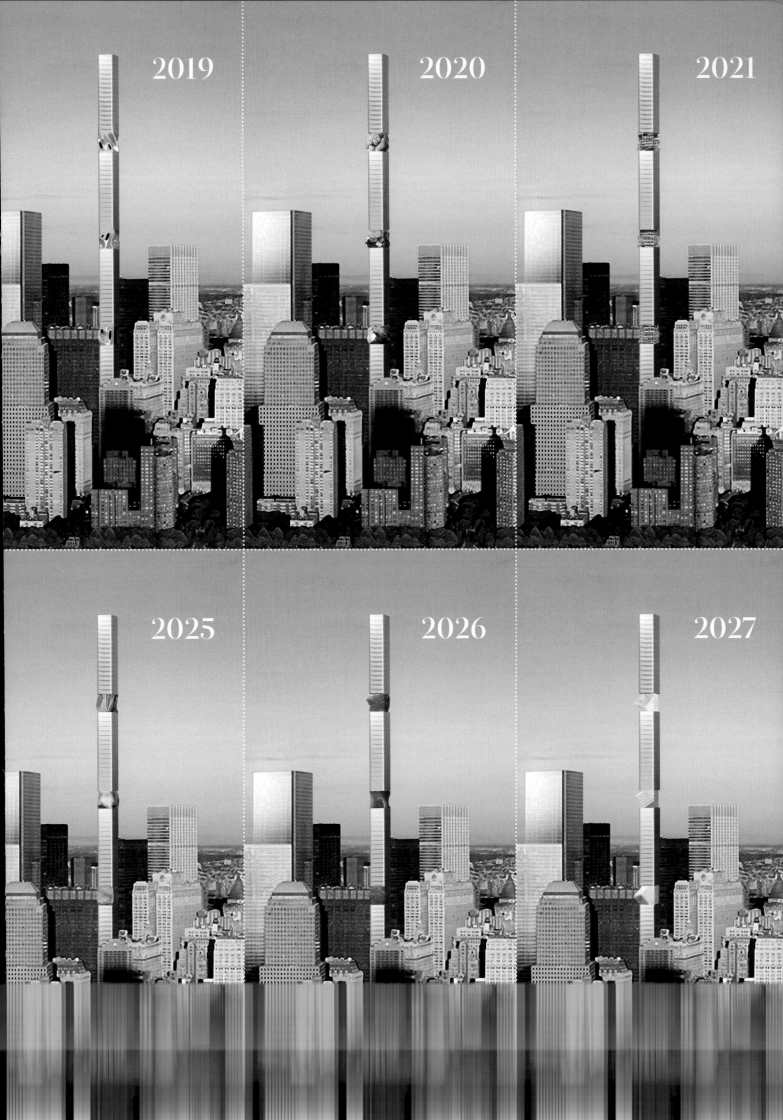

2019　　　2020　　　2021

2025　　　2026　　　2027

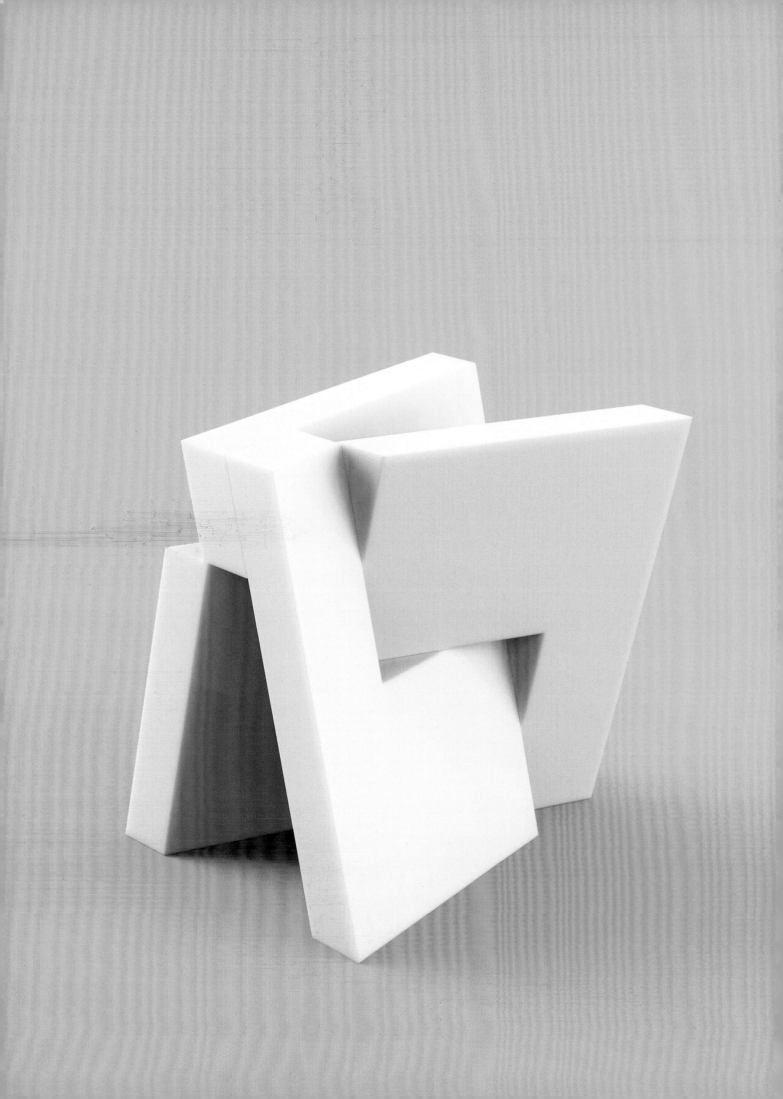

QuaDror

Can a new geometry revolutionize how we build?

QuaDror has been one of our studio's biggest passions. Funny enough though, it may never have come to be had it not been for one serendipitous discovery. It all started when we were approached by the crystal elements-licensing arm of Swarovski, Crystallized, to create a design using their crystals, and we decided to make a chandelier. Traditionally, a chandelier hangs in the center of a room, usually above a table, defining an axis of symmetry for all the other elements in the room. Our natural instinct kicked in, and not wanting to fulfill most of the typical expectations of what a chandelier is, we imagined one that would sit off-center to the room, over to the side, and on the floor.

Our idea was to create two square frames that inter-sected diagonally with each other. The space between them would be woven with wires, forming a parabolic net that would in turn hold the Swarovski crystals. We assembled a large team and spent a very long week-end stringing crystals—about 7,000 overall—by hand.

Before the final assembly, while I was experimenting in the workshop, making a small operable prototype, I discovered something. If I broke down the two squares into four identical L-shaped pieces, with identical beveled edges, and arranged them together, it would not only reform the two squares, but also form a new type of structure.

For many days after we had this prototype sitting on our table. We toyed with it, opening and closing it, wondering: what are we going to do with this?

We became obsessed.

We gave it a name: QuaDror.

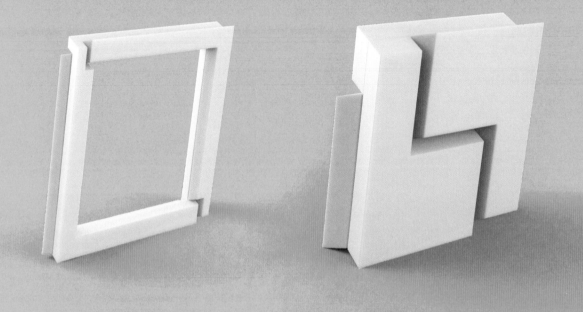

How to build QuaDror

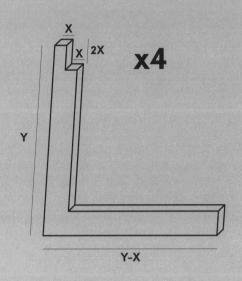

x4

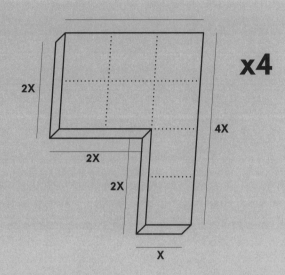

x4

1. 4 Identical L-shaped pieces, with beveled edges.
2. The angle of the bevel will dictate how much the QuaDror opens. The angle of the L-member will dictate the appearance of the QuaDror element.
3. Lay flat two L-shapes to form a solid square. Make sure the beveled edges touch and leave no gaps. (x2)
4. Flip one of the squares over and rotate 90° and lay over the other square.
5. Connect each L-shaped piece to its opposite, via the two overlapping areas.
6. Rotate and open. Voilà!

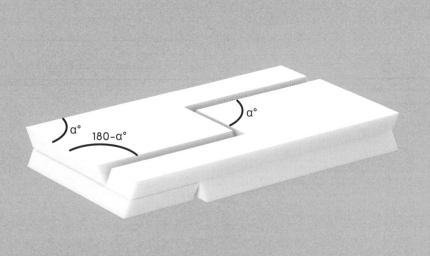

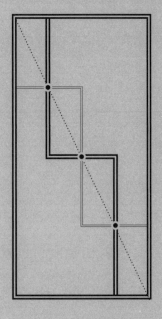

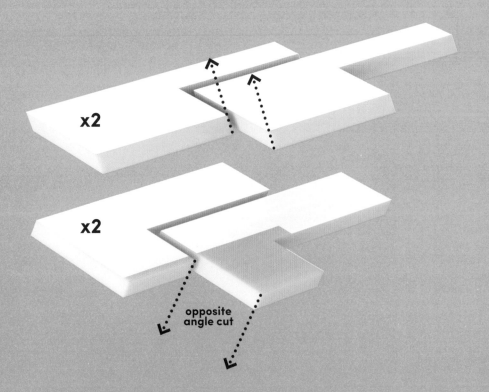

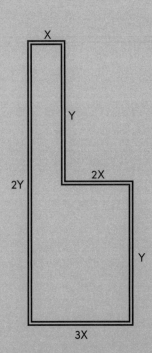

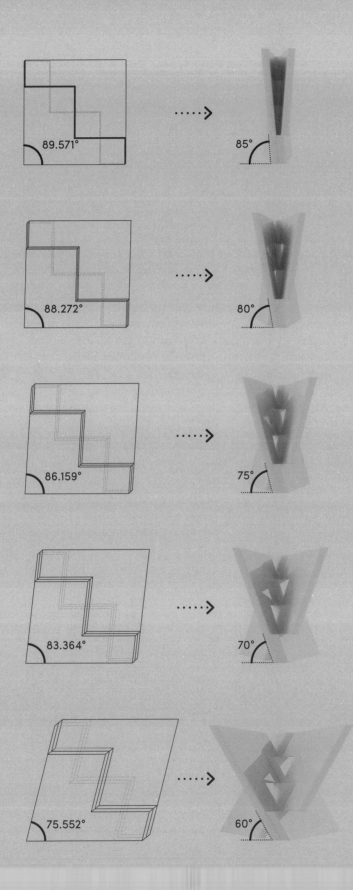

89.571° ·····> 85°

88.272° ·····> 80°

86.159° ·····> 75°

83.364° ·····> 70°

75.552° ·····> 60°

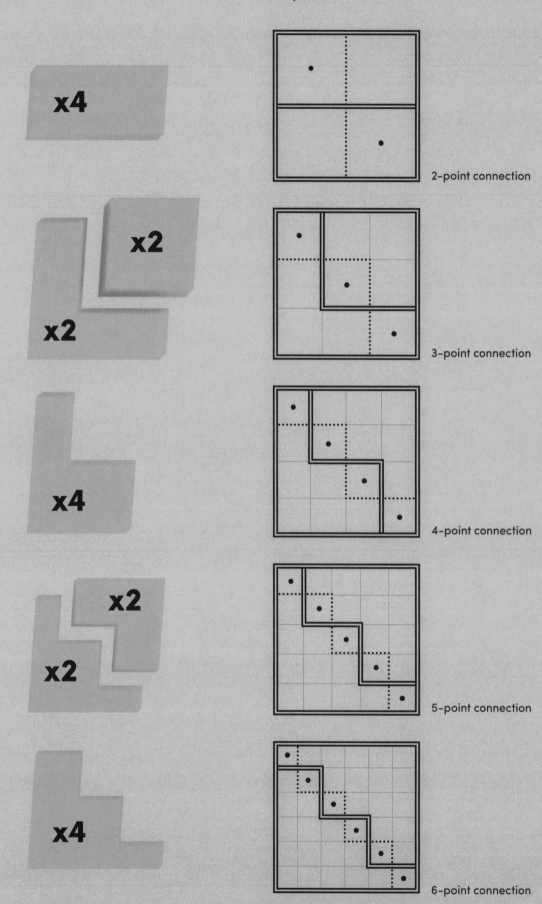

2-point connection

3-point connection

4-point connection

5-point connection

6-point connection

QuaDror

 x2

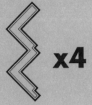 **x4**

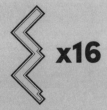 **x16**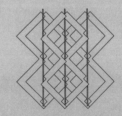

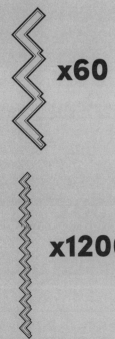 **x60**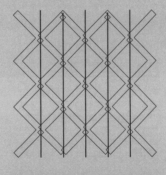

x1200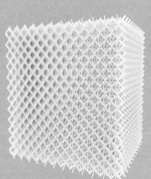

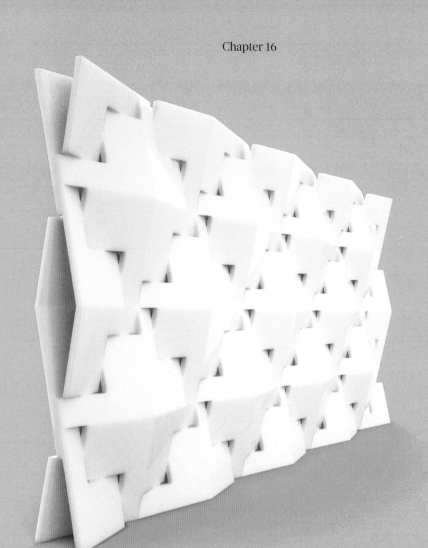

Closed system

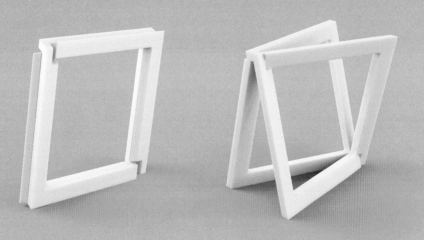

Open system

Had we re-discovered something existing or was it truly new?

Our newfound obsession begged this and many other questions. In order to answer them we undertook a great deal of research and experimentation. We looked at past work, searched for natural precedents, and were confident that we had discovered something novel. As we investigated further, we realized that while QuaDror is essentially a joint without a pin, this range of operability allowed it to

be both easily transported—essentially flat-packed—when closed, and incredibly structurally strong once opened.

When we started thinking about all the possibilities, we were blown away. It was certainly strong enough to hold a table, a bookcase, but why stop there. Imagine what else it could support? And not only that, how fast could it be deployed? Could it reduce construction time and labor? Could it be used to raise a tower in no time? Could it be

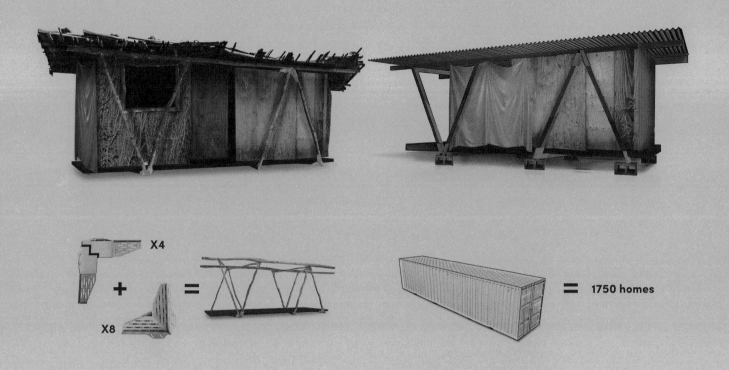

X4

X8

= 1750 homes

deployed to disaster zones as relief shelter? Could it help solve housing shortages around the world? Its potential and versatility inspired us to explore and further manipulate as many of QuaDror's design variables as we could. So far we had discovered its great physical strength and easy deployability, but what other properties were waiting to be discovered? What else was possible?

We resolved to build as many models as we could, at varying scales and in different materials. We

explored stacking and aggregating QuaDror units, and the different ways of securing them to each other. We created two versions: "Open" (open-frame), and "Closed" (closed-planar).

All of these models helped us immensely to understand the geometric, scalar, and material versatility of QuaDror. We developed a remarkable body of research and knew that if we wanted to find out more we needed to find the best engineers and consultants. We

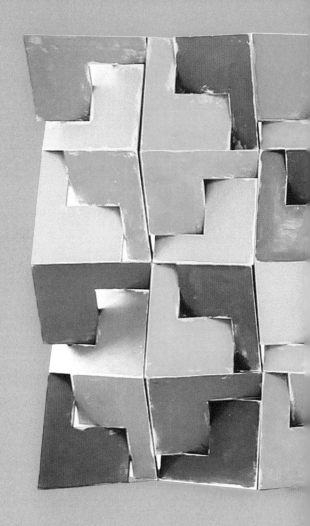

gathered some preliminary data, but what was the precise way forward? To approach different specialized companies based on the different applications we envisioned, one by one? Start with small-scale applications first and then build up? Or vice versa? Or perhaps simply to begin with an art installation?

We didn't know the answers to these questions, so we decided to sidestep them. Instead of knocking on endless doors seeking collaborators,

we would let them seek us out. We decided to share our discoveries and launch a press campaign. After searching for the right event to debut QuaDror, we decided on Design Indaba.

It was 2011. Our communications director, Melanie Courbet, coordinated a fantastic campaign; at the same moment I went on stage at Design Indaba, *Fast Company*, *Huffington Post*, *The New York Times*, *CNN* and *Wallpaper** magazine also launched QuaDror live on their websites. It was brilliant.

I look back at Design Indaba 2011 as one of the most memorable and amazing conferences we have ever attended. We made a lot of good friends, still to this day. And the launch campaign was extremely successful. Our inbox flooded with emails from governments, public institutions, and NGOs; from different individuals, companies, and manufacturers all the way from Russia to Ethiopia. The enthusiasm and response was so varied that we were overwhelmed; yet again we didn't know what to prioritize.

It was a bittersweet moment, one of our biggest successes yet at the same time one of our biggest mistakes. It was also our best learning experience. Everyone was asking us for prices, delivery times, turnaround times—but we didn't have a product ready for sale. We just had ideas that needed further research and development into their viability. We told everyone inquiring about our situation, and 90 percent of them gave us a number to contact them when QuaDror would be ready.

Our excellent PR campaign had created an immense enthusiasm for QuaDror, but failed to communicate our basic intent: to find collaborators. Everyone wanted the product but no one wanted to help us to research and develop it. By this time, we had exhausted ourselves and decided to let QuaDror rest for a while. We had learned an invaluable lesson: to move forward we needed to prioritize and make a plan, we needed to zoom out. We needed a global picture.

After giving it some time and thought we decided that the first step forward was to categorize the wealth of knowledge we had developed so far. In doing so, we hoped to not only see the breadth of our research through a new lens, but also to develop a strategy to focus our next steps. Indeed, after looking at our research arrayed in this fashion, it became apparent that QuaDror existed in two slightly different applications: either as an open or a closed system.

These two categories allowed us to organize and divide our future explorations. It allowed us to consolidate our 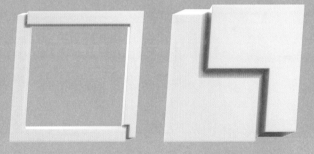 research efforts, since all experiments in each category share inherent properties, but, additionally, it also allowed us to better explore their related practical applications. That is to say, we could pool research that explored the structural performance of QuaDror as an open system, and use it to inves-tigate applications of QuaDror from sawhorse to a building's structural frame.

2007 **Swarovski Crystallized**

2007 **Sawhorses**

2007 **Wall**

2011 **Relief Housing**

2011 **New Museum**

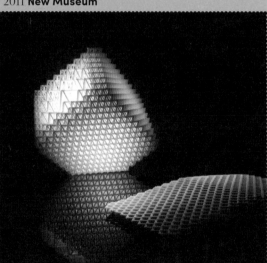

2011 **Highway Barrier**

2011 **Interni**

2009 **Volume.MGX**

2012 **Popup Pavilion**

2012 **Reach**

2015 **Bookcase**

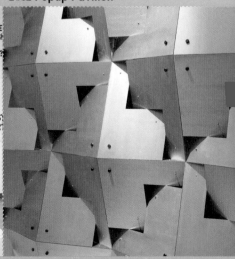

2015 **Room Divider**

2008 **Foundation of Knowledge**

2009 **Yigal Azrouël**

2010 **Design Indaba**

2010 **Guggenheim**

2008 **Houses**

2010 **Puma**

2012 **Cut25**

2013 **WeWork**

2013 **MoMA PS1**

What follows here is a brief history of our most memorable QuaDror explorations seen through this lens.

Closed system

QuaDror as a closed system is in essence just the pure structural hinge unencumbered. When we first scaled this hinge to a larger yet still maneuverable size, we realized that if we aggregated several units horizontally, and stacked them on top of one another, we could form a wall. This QuaDror wall, with its jagged geometry, hinted at a wealth of properties, from sound proofing to optical and kinetic effects.

As is often the case with our experiments, we first started to explore these wall aggregations through art installations and exhibitions. These events, with their brief turnaround time, were ideal for quick tests in program and materiality.

In fact, we had previously fabricated some QuaDror units for an exhibition curated by Luminaire in Design Miami 2008. The exhibition was titled *Paperlove* and asked us to review the role of paper in our current era. Paper, a remarkable technological breakthrough when introduced long ago, had surely taken on a different role with the introduction of digital culture, the internet, Google,

and wikis. We sought to transform the obsolete
relevance of physical reference books, such
as encyclopedias, dictionaries, and atlases, by
recasting them as physical QuaDror structures.
We called our entry *The Foundation of Knowledge.*

While this exhibition prompted us to keep exploring
the material possibilities for QuaDror, it also
revealed the power of QuaDror as a sculptural and
performative object. We took these ideas to heart
as we oversaw the art direction for fashion designer
Yigal Azrouël's Fall 2009 Men's collection. The show,
a live performance by the models, incorporated
the on-stage assembly of thirty-two solid QuaDror
elements, stacked to form a wall. These QuaDror
elements were made of MDF and presented

both flat and assembled. When assembled they showcased a painting by the artist Dov Talpaz, whose prints also appeared on some of the clothing. The live construction and deconstruction of the wall highlighted Yigal's attention to details and layers.

Afterwards, at Salone del Mobile 2011 in Milan, the Italian publication *Interni* invited us to participate in their exhibition *Mutant Architecture & Design* at the Università degli Studi di Milano. Together with a selection of designers—including Zaha Hadid,

Ingo Maurer, and Carlo Colombo—we were asked to offer examples of "mutant architecture": highly flexible structures that could be easily be dismantled, rebuilt, moved, and modified to various locations and contexts over time. The long, majestic space presented a natural opportunity to further our research in the fabrication of QuaDror, and we built thirty units with a concrete finish with the Italian fabricator Moretti. The resulting four walls showed the adaptability of QuaDror, each demonstrating a different configuration.

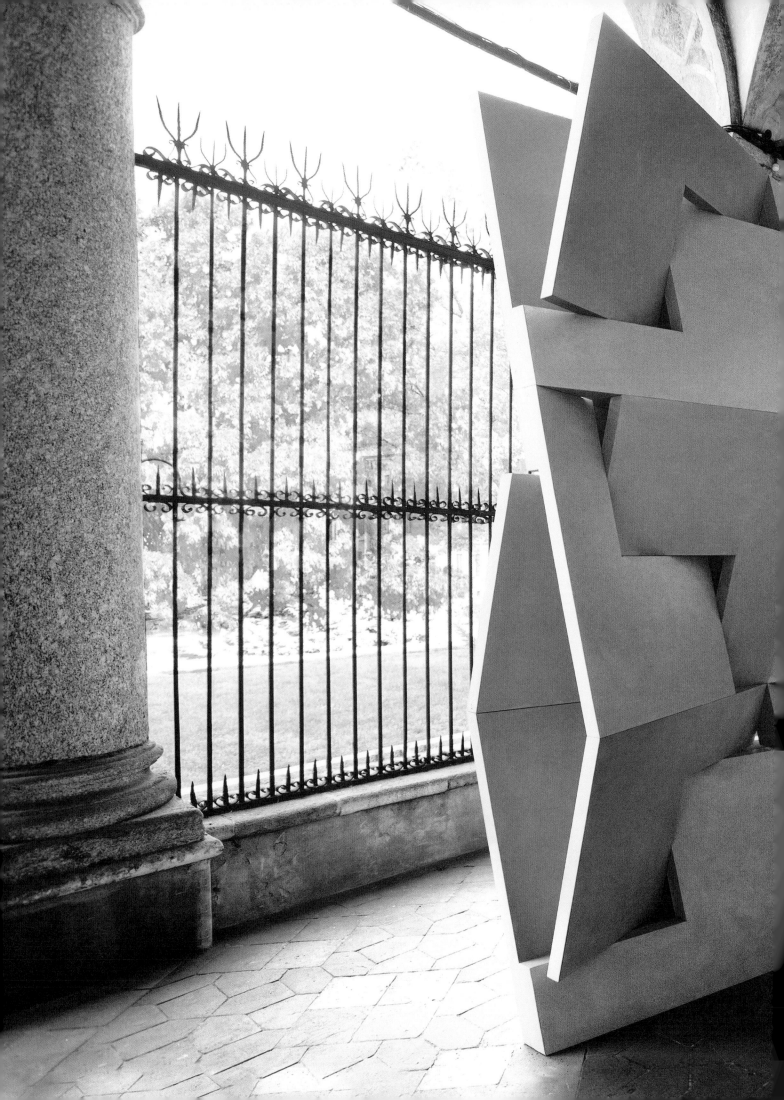

Red markings capture
the movement of a Continuous

At this stage, most of our explorations were made of some form of wood or composite, and usually hand-crafted. As we sought out other materials to fabricate from, we also became increasingly curious about the possibilities of digital fabrication. This was especially key as we researched fabricating QuaDror from stainless steel; we realized that the thickness we wanted to achieve was close to impossible with nominal gauges. We did some research and found a company called Industrial Origami, whose folding technology allowed us

to form folded QuaDror units out of one sheet of metal. The resulting prototype maintained structural strength and efficiency, but by using a single sheet, it was also lightweight. The reduced amount of material and welding labor made its fabrication very energy efficient.

In 2012, when we were approached to participate in an exhibition curated and produced by Love & Art Children's Foundation at the Brazilian Museum of Sculpture in São Paulo, we partnered with Mekal and Aperam to produce a sculpture inspired by our new prototype. The resulting 5-meter high sculpture, *Reach*, consisted of fifteen QuaDrors arranged as an open stairway stretching toward the sky. After the exhibition, the sculpture was donated and relocated to a school in the south of Brazil, where the composition aimed to inspire the young students.

Working with folded steel had been driven by the constraint of stacking. Simply put, conventional steel gauges were too thin to be able to stack properly. But, because in our research applications we had opened the doors to techniques such as metal jet cutting and laser cutting, we endeavored to find a way to develop QuaDror units of a thin gauge material thickness. Using the techniques we had previously learned, we designed a QuaDror unit of single-sheet thickness that could be assembled and aggregated with simple fasteners. This last prototype helped inform our Room Divider, produced as part of the larger QuaDror furniture collection launched in 2015.

Over the past few years we have made plenty of headway in material and fabrication research

Arminda - década de 80
Sonia Ehling
doação da artista

regarding our closed QuaDror systems. Recently, we decided to combine our collected research, move beyond unique sculptural pieces, and seek applications that take advantage of all of QuaDror's properties. Aesthetically engaging, structurally strong, with great sound reflection capacities, and, of course, easy to assemble, QuaDror is a natural replacement for traditional construction barriers. Current ground-up construction projects in the studio, like Galata Grounds (Chapter 26), will be proving grounds for QuaDror Barriers.

Open system

In contrast to closed and solid QuaDror applications, which excel as either freestanding objects or space dividers, open systems are ideally suited to become load-bearing frames capable of supporting any flat surface, from tabletops to roofs.

Indeed, our serendipitous discovery of QuaDror came while constructing a frame. As we began

to analyze it and became aware of its structural strength, our first resolve was to create a saw-horse capable of serving as the base for a table. As we continued to research, exploring QuaDror's effectiveness in furniture was simply irresistible.

Over the years we developed many designs and applications, some of which we even used in our custom retail projects, from display shelves to clothing racks. It was not until 2015, when in collaboration with Italian manufacturer Horm, we debuted the first QuaDror Furniture collection. Using noble and elegant materials, the series introduced QuaDror to the domestic environment.

At the same time, we also researched larger-scale applications. We began by designing a flexible housing system which would utilize QuaDror as its structural frame. These frames were to be prefabricated using laminated beams connected with custom steel hinges. Given the collapsibility of QuaDror, we envisioned that the house could be shipped flat. On site, the structural units could be erected and secured, allowing the rest of the house and finishes to follow.

We learned a good deal from our first foray into QuaDror as a building frame. The system had immense structural potential, and while we were not ready to explore the prefab market, we could not shy away from the system's potential for quick deployability. In order to further investigate this aspect, we chose to focus on two potential applications: a temporary pavilion and relief housing.

In 2010, the ideal opportunity arose to explore the former. Puma approached us to propose a new design for its yearly traveling pavilion. Their most recent structure had been made of shipping containers, which was novel but still a major

QuaDror

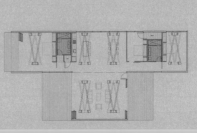

operation to assemble, disassemble, and transport because each volume had to be overtly reinforced. We were confident that using QuaDror frames would be ideal to create a lighter and efficient customizable pavilion.

We proposed a 12,000 square-foot building made from seventy-nine identical QuaDror frames made with standard I-beams, connected with custom QuaDror hinges. The frames were in turn blanketed on one side with architectural fabric,

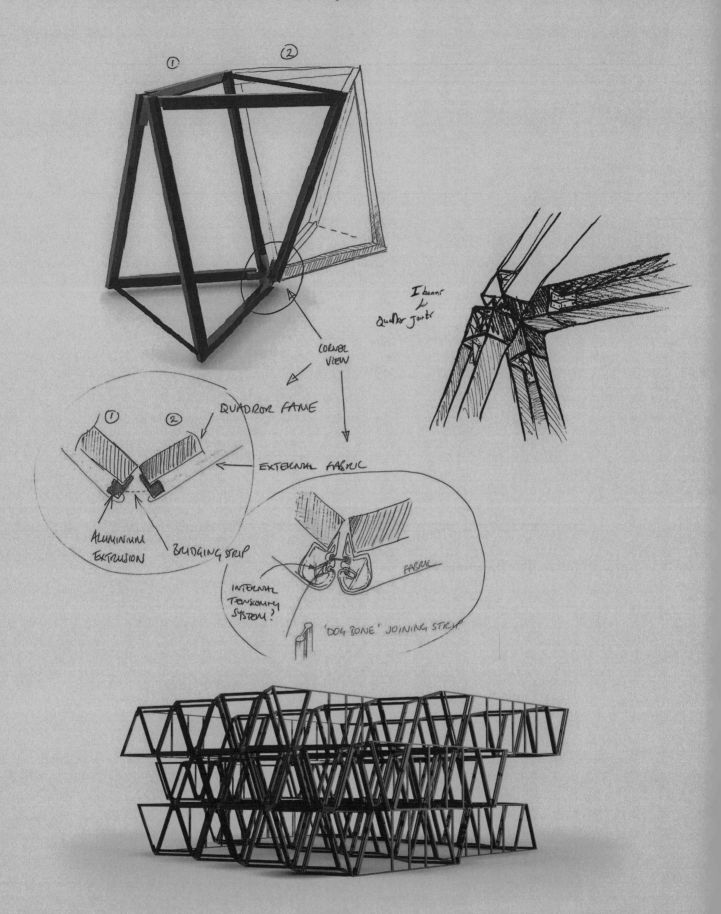

① ②

I beams
&
Quador Joints

CORNER
VIEW

QUADROR FRAME

① ②

EXTERNAL FABRIC

ALUMINIUM
EXTRUSION

BRIDGING STRIP

INTERNAL
TENSIONING
SYSTEM?

FABRIC

'DOG BONE' JOINING STRIP

while the remaining sides of the pavilion were to be covered with glazing panels. All elements considered, the structure could be easily packaged into just ten shipping containers, and assembled on-site. On every assembly, the pavilion could be easily modified to adapt to the different plots; it was a blank canvas for events, pop-up shops, or temporary installations.

In order to properly engineer these QuaDror frames we partnered with the global engineering

firm Arup. The analyses done by their team proved invaluable to our further understanding of the structural performance of QuaDror. And it also paved the way for our experiments into short-term disaster-relief housing.

In the Puma pavilion we had separated the QuaDror frame into simple I-beams connected to custom hinges, essentially creating a kit of parts. If we could further simplify and standardize these elements, this new kit could not only provide a safer and

stronger option to most relief housing, but it could also be just as easily deployed in needed areas worldwide. Combining standard wood beams with a modified custom QuaDror joint, we aimed to use as little material as possible to enclose the largest amount of area, in the most efficient way, and at a minimal cost.

By providing an easy, self-assembled and adaptable option, we hoped to not only provide shelter, but also to inspire hope and improve lives. We exhibited these designs for QuaDror Relief Housing as part of the US QuaDror debut at New York's New Museum in 2011, and we submitted it as part of MoMA PS1's 2013 Rockaways Call for Ideas. Our proposal envisioned a structural system that could act as a blank canvas, provi-ding the community with a maximum variety of uses which they themselves could define to address their specific needs.

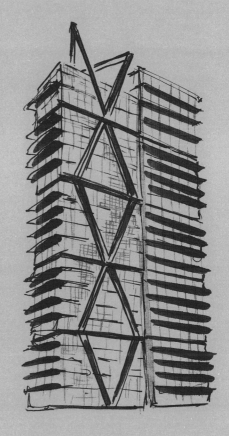

These initial architectural investigations led the way for us to envision even larger QuaDror applications. When we were approached to design a tower for 100 Varick in New York City, we developed a QuaDror exoskeleton, which replaced the interior support system of a traditional high-rise, allowing glass volumes to be inserted into the apertures formed by the frame. Totaling twenty-five stories, the structure is efficiently divided into independent five-story units. By placing the supporting framework on the outside, the building becomes refreshingly open, providing uninterrupted living spaces for its tenants.

At first it was certainly unimaginable that the design of a chandelier could, in the future, also become

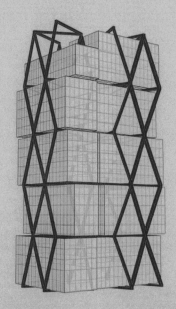
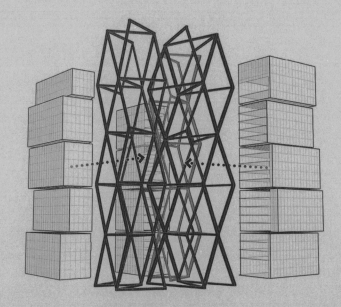

the exoskeleton of a residential tower. The power of QuaDror as an easily deployable structural hinge had opened a world of promise for us.

Indeed, in 2009, when 3D-printing manufacturer Materialise approached us to create something for their MGX collection, we saw the opportunity to take QuaDror to new territories. If we were to aggregate QuaDror frames in two directions and rotate them, we would have in our hands a volumetric space frame. And given the capacity

of 3D printing to build ready-assembled volumes, we aggregated the biggest number of QuaDrors to date: 1,200 units. These units intersect to form a truncated cube; now it's a lamp shade for a light placed within.

As we continued to discover yet more design possibilities for QuaDror, it seemed only fitting that we should find a way to systematize it, variable by variable, and develop our own digital tool. As our team grew, so did our knowledge of parametric

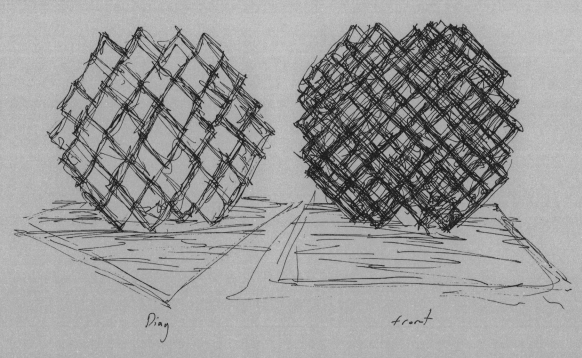

Diag   front

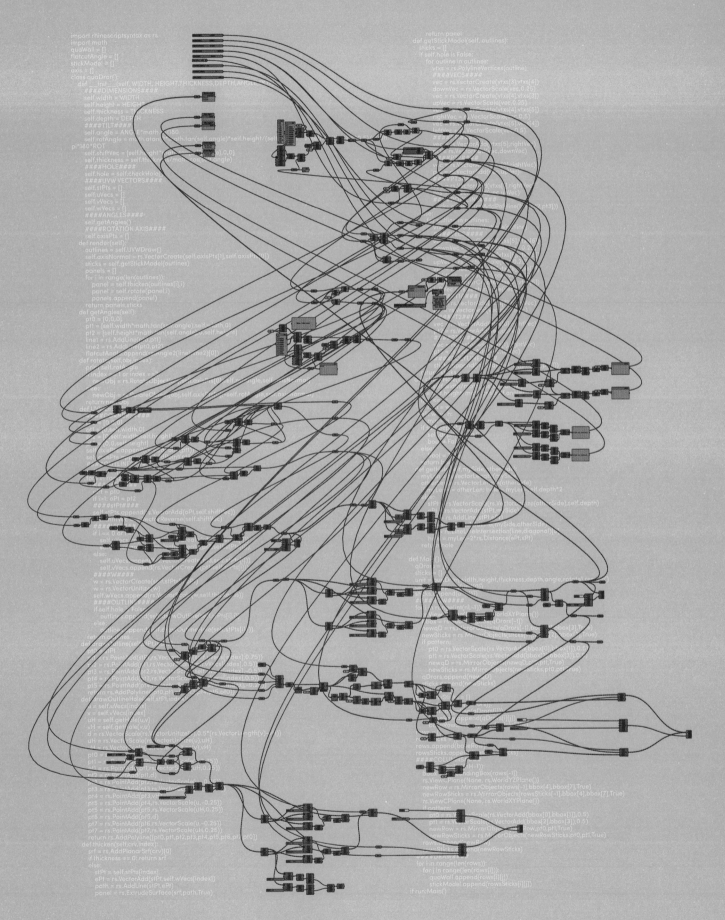

tools and software, and our very own QuaDror Grasshopper widget came to be.

At this time, the New Zealand wine producer Brancott Estate approached the studio after they'd seen our work online. They invited us to visit their vineyards in Marlborough and translate its spirit into a new form through design. We explored the limits of our new tool to design a QuaDror volume that not only adjusted to the size of the lot, but also allowed us to calculate the amount of material needed and maintain our design within the budget. We also smoothly translated the nine-meter-tall sculptural volume into a functional, smaller-scale wine rack made of electro-coated steel. This sculpture will be the beginning of many QuaDror spaces to come.

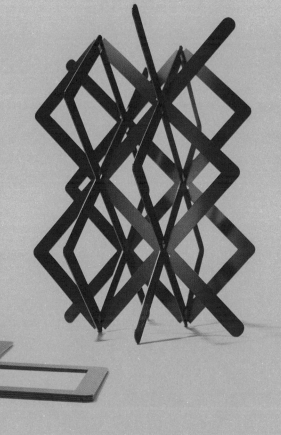

In order to fully understand something, one has to build it and stand up under it.
—Buckminster Fuller

Chapter 17
National Library of Israel

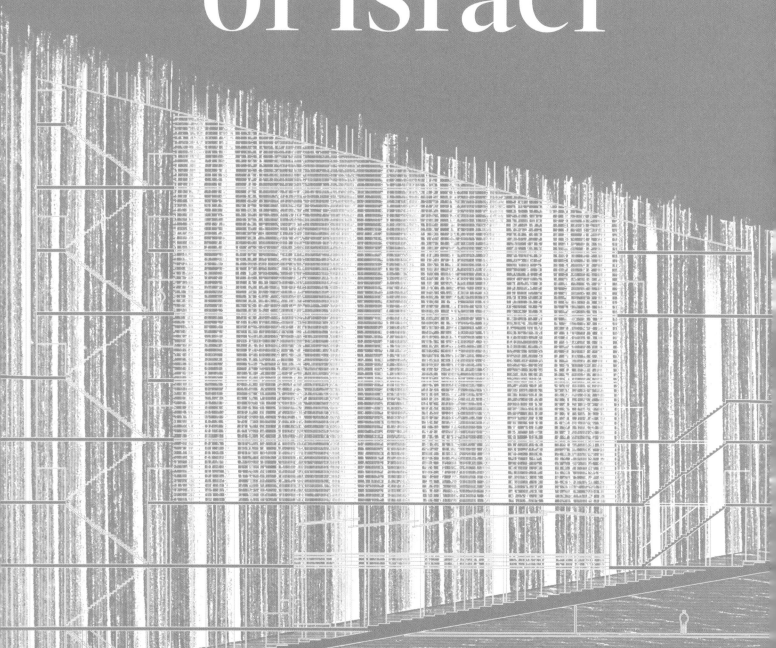

The eye is the window to the mind.

The National Library of Israel is one of the most important archives of literature and ancient religious scripts in the world, and home to an incredible collection of more than five million books, in addition to numerous rare manuscripts and artifacts. As part of its renewal process, the institution launched a design competition to create an expanded facility for the twenty-first century. As we began considering what this kind of archive of information represented, we

Going up
Education

Going down
Knowledge

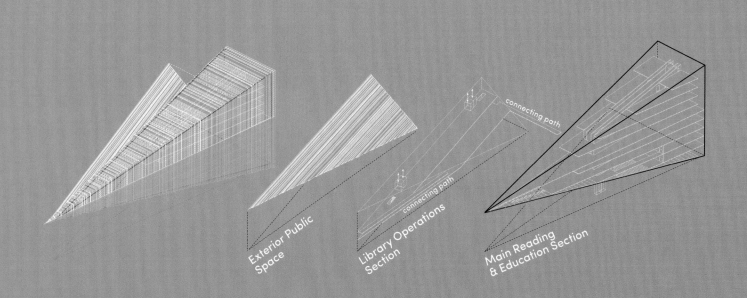

Exterior Public
Space

Library Operations
Section

connecting path

Main Reading
& Education Section

connecting path

looked at the idea of knowledge, at how we perceive and interact with it. And it was the idea that the eye is the window to the mind that was the starting point of our design motivations. I began thinking about the relationship between these texts and the human eye, the first tool used to process words. I wanted to create a building that symbolized this internalization —a gradually increasing aggregation of knowledge.

The idea was that the building starts at a little point, a stone, and grows in scale to a large proportion, maintaining a symmetrical section and plan. Half of the library goes down into the earth and the other goes up into the sky—a metaphor for gaining knowledge, digging deeper or climbing higher and higher. The most literal, geometric representation of this relationship is a square-base pyramid. We rotated, or tipped, this pyramid so it rests on a flat triangular face, and this new orientation informed the edifice of the building. We aimed to give the facades the look of paper, with striated cuts in the Jerusalem stone to suggest the pages in a book, layers of information laid with stone.

That was how we organized the library and the structure. Together, the library's vertical and horizontal movements encapsulate the depth of meaning and mental elevation acquired through reading in a physical form.

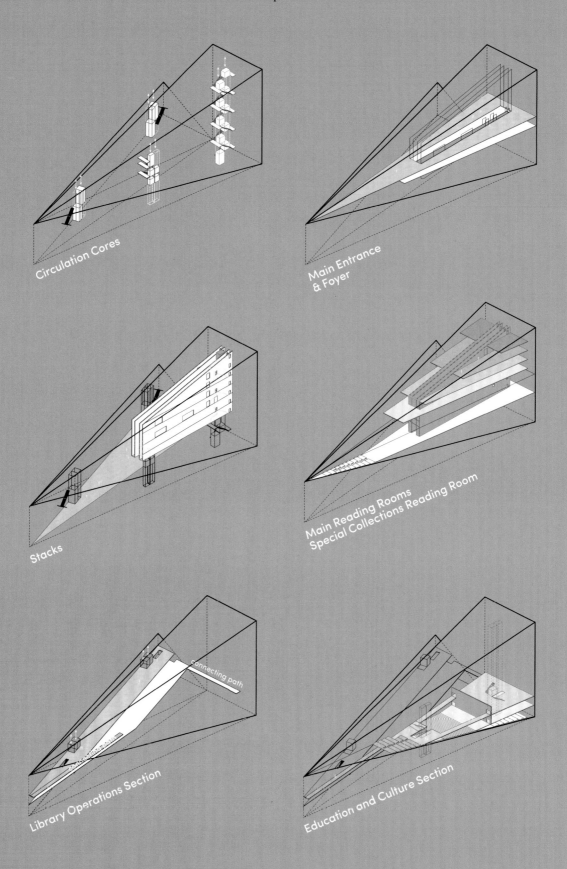

Circulation Cores

Main Entrance
& Foyer

Stacks

Main Reading Rooms
Special Collections Reading Room

Connecting path

Library Operations Section

Education and Culture Section

Miami Lift

Creating strength from a single fold.

The 2013 DawnTown Landmark Miami competition focused on the phenomenon of branding a city with instantly recognizable structures. Miami already has its share of existing local landmarks, but as the city changes, the competition organizers wanted design-ers to come up with a new symbol for the future. The competition outlined creating an iconic architectural work that contributes to the image of Miami.

Miami is the US gateway to Latin America and the Caribbean; it's also known as the cruise ship mecca of the world. So the idea of Miami as an entrance and a hub for water transportation was something that influenced us to think about a building that presented itself as a ship if you were to see it from the water, but as a rising landform looking from the city out to the water. The lower floors would address programmatic needs and also position it in this space, but it would look like the building was lifting away from the earth, creating a new mini-

Urban link

Flagler St. axis is an urban link between the city and the water.

Water connection

The Noguchi fountain site has a special potential to connect the city to its waterfront.

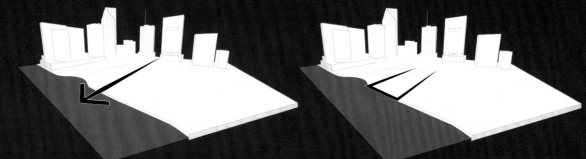

harbor underneath. The idea of building something that peels itself off the earth's surface and utilizes the strength of a fold was interesting to the studio. A single fold is the easiest way to create strength in any sheet material. If you take a piece of paper and you want to stiffen it, create one fold or crease. The structure of Miami Lift creates a gesture of welcoming and ascendance.

Lift & reveal

Lifting the land reveals a new relationship between the park and the bay.

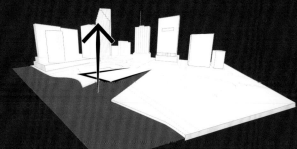

Fold open

The lifted tower creates new programmatic potential in the park, as well as a landmark that dwells along the water's edge.

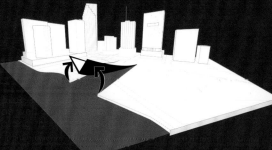

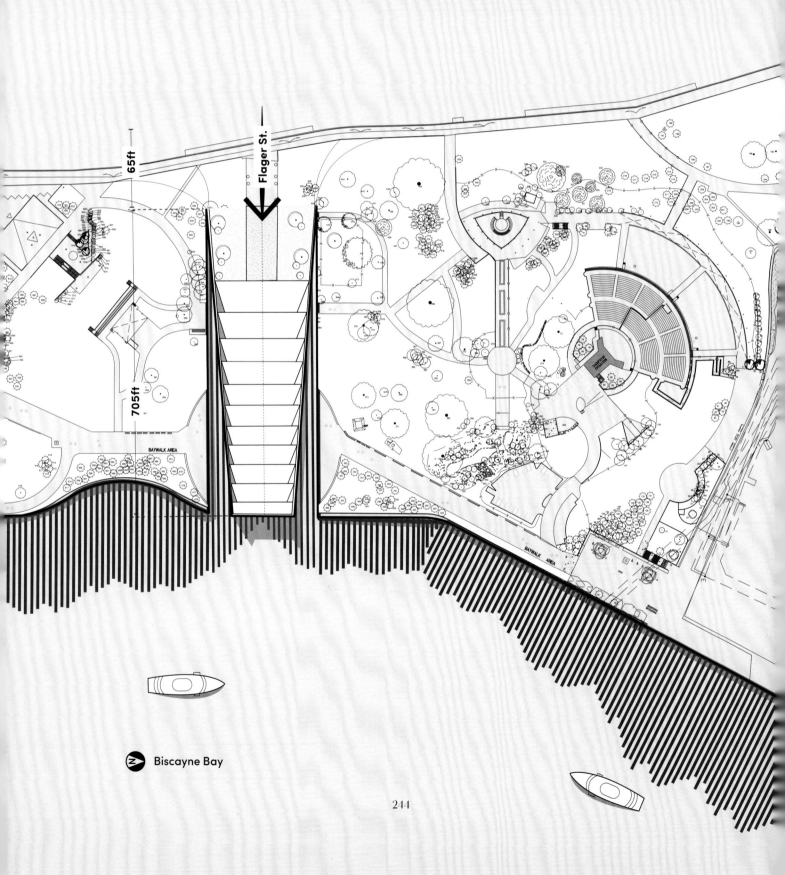

65ft

Flager St.

705ft

BAYWALK AREA

BAYWALK AREA

Biscayne Bay

Miami's extensive beaches, unique culture, and prime location for cruise travel come together to create a cohesive identity. Miami Lift pays tribute to this by elevating visitors, and giving them a new perspective of the city.

We won first prize for this unbuilt design competition project.

....

Miami Lift

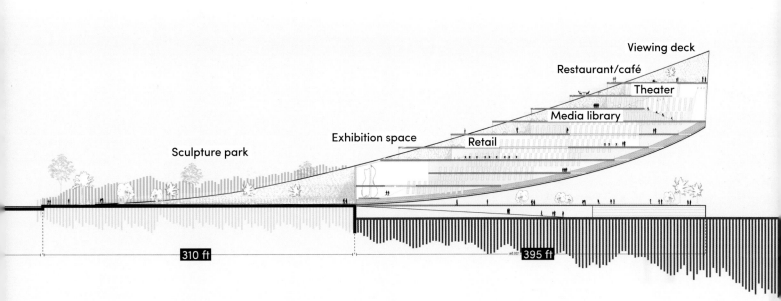

Viewing deck

Restaurant/café

Theater

Media library

Exhibition space

Retail

Sculpture park

310 ft

395 ft

Chapter 19

Istanbul Modern

A suspended expression by the Bosphorus.

The Istanbul Modern Art Museum, the most important contemporary art museum in the city, directly fronts the Bosphorus River on a site that we are extensively redeveloping, Galata Grounds (Chapter 26). The museum's story is an inspiring tale: despite the problematic issues contemporary art presents to the region, one family's dream

to create a sustained presence for art in the city prevailed. In our proposal for the institution's renovation, creating a new facade that honored this enduring achievement was paramount.

We began thinking about the relationship between modern art and its artists, and how we might relate that to a structure that sits on the historic Bosphorus. Art conjures up the idea of a suspended expression—a split second held at a standstill. A fountain, for example, could

be represented as a motionless, elevated mass. This notion of art suspending an experience in motion formed the foundation of our concept.

The studio's proposal for the Istanbul Modern starts with a minimal white rectangle, which, like contemporary galleries, aims to compete as little as possible with the art inside. Surrounding the structure is a layer of narrow, tendril-like shoots of stacked, structurally independent fragments of bleached concrete. The shoots extend to various heights, evoking a fountain frozen in time. A slit of glass peeks through the top of the museum's boardwalk-facing side, providing sweeping views for a terrace or café.

Chapter 20

Guggenheim Helsinki

Creating a gallery in the forest; an ever-changing cultural icon.

The studio entered a competition held for the new location of the Guggenheim Museum in Helsinki; the process of developing our submission was fascinating for a lot of different reasons. I started by thinking about how museums often double as architectural icons, where a building is synonymous with its designer. Certain iconic buildings become

associated with an architect's name; with the Guggenheim Helsinki, could we challenge that relationship between the name of a building and the presence and life of the building? And why would a museum which changes curatorial content constantly need to have the same physical presence all the time? This approach demonstrates the disconnect between the exterior's messaging and the exhibitions inside—a shared dialogue around art is missing. I wanted to create a museum that could celebrate its ever-changing content on its facade: a performing

monument to art. It was also important that the structure resonate with its surroundings in the Finnish capital in a distinctive and meaningful way.

But how could we make a building actually change its look based on the content of the exhibitions inside? We found a newly invented glass technology called OLED, which in one mode is a clear panel, but also has the ability to become a screen. Of course the possibilities are endless, from a structure that appears completely transparent to one that looks and behaves in different ways, seemingly shifting its physical form to reflect its interior mood.

We began with a minimal rectangular building wrapped in thin OLED panels that could project imagery and act as a curated extension of the exhibitions inside. We also surrounded the building with a strategically arranged grid of birch trees. The vegetation softens and camouflages the building's sharp edges, creating an optical illusion of a structure that magically dissolves into the

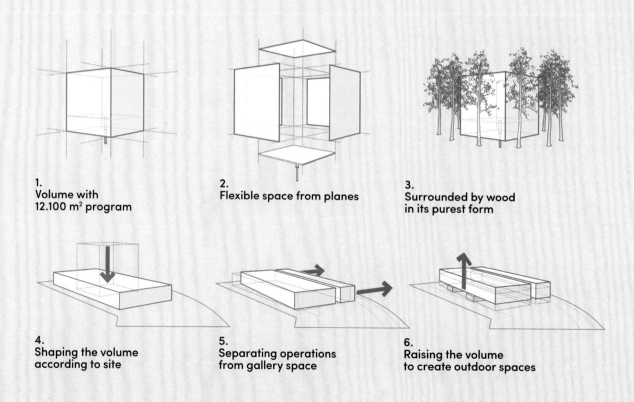

1.
Volume with
12.100 m² program

2.
Flexible space from planes

3.
Surrounded by wood
in its purest form

4.
Shaping the volume
according to site

5.
Separating operations
from gallery space

6.
Raising the volume
to create outdoor spaces

manufactured forest. "Cladding" the museum with nature was important for different reasons: one, to honor the four full seasons around the building, and allow it to interact with the trees. And second, to camouflage the building in such a way that you don't just see a square screen but you can actually play with shapes that are hidden between the trees and change the appearance of the building, make it look like it doesn't exist, blur the edges of the building...and using that logic, also change the dimension of the spaces.

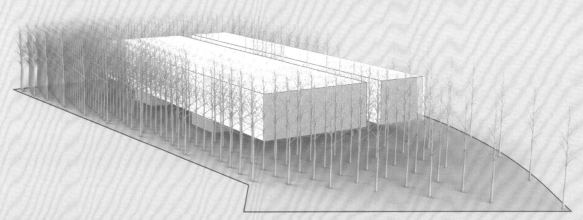

7.
Man-made forest

Scenario 1
Anish Kapoor

Scenario 2
Tomás Saraceno

Summer
Light Shading

Scenario 3
Cai Guo-Qiang

Scenario 4
James Turrell

Winter
Maximum Exposure

Can a building actually change its look based on the content of the exhibition inside?

Longitudinal section

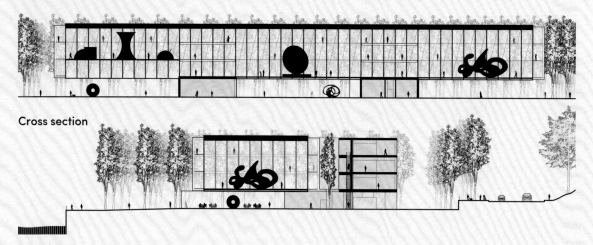

Cross section

Inside, three lightweight, minimal platforms can be adjusted to multiple heights to complement artworks of varying scales. This system provides yet another flexible element of the building and allows the art to assert itself on the interior, allowing artists and curators to create an exhibition space customized for the objects it presents.

By establishing a dialogue between the museum's interior and exterior, as well as its surroundings, our concept for the Guggenheim Helsinki ushers in a third voice: nature.

With each season, the Nordic woods provide another constantly changing layer to consider in curating content for the facade.

....

Guggenheim Helsinki

Program

Museum levels
& moving platforms

M Mechanical room
S Storage closet
WC Bathrooms
FE Freight elevator
KE Kitchen elevator
E Escalator

01. Security
02. Staff lockers
03. Custodial
04. Landscape & grounds
maintenance equipment
05. Supply, equipment
& seasonal furniture storage
06. Stock room
07. Visitor screening / bag check
08. Coat check

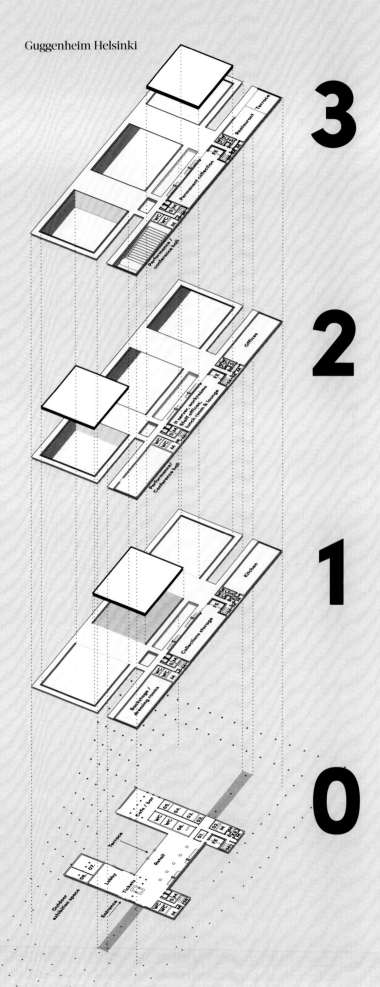

3

2

1

0

Exhibition framework

The building is split into two volumes in order to
alleviate the exhibition spaces from operations, thus
creating a blank canvas for accentuated curatorial
and artistic interventions.

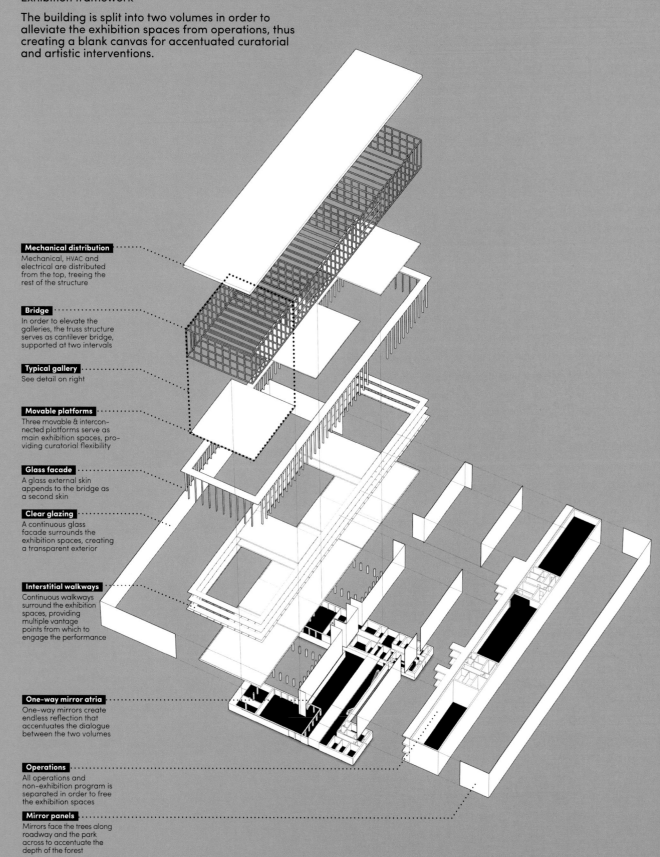

Mechanical distribution
Mechanical, HVAC and
electrical are distributed
from the top, treeing the
rest of the structure

Bridge
In order to elevate the
galleries, the truss structure
serves as cantilever bridge,
supported at two intervals

Typical gallery
See detail on right

Movable platforms
Three movable & intercon-
nected platforms serve as
main exhibition spaces, providing curatorial flexibility

Glass facade
A glass external skin
appends to the bridge as
a second skin

Clear glazing
A continuous glass
facade surrounds the
exhibition spaces, creating
a transparent exterior

Interstitial walkways
Continuous walkways
surround the exhibition
spaces, providing
multiple vantage
points from which to
engage the performance

One-way mirror atria
One-way mirrors create
endless reflection that
accentuates the dialogue
between the two volumes

Operations
All operations and
non-exhibition program is
separated in order to free
the exhibition spaces

Mirror panels
Mirrors face the trees along
roadway and the park
across to accentuate the
depth of the forest

Typical gallery

Movable platform with surrounding walkways
connected to 3 storey interconnecting gallery volume

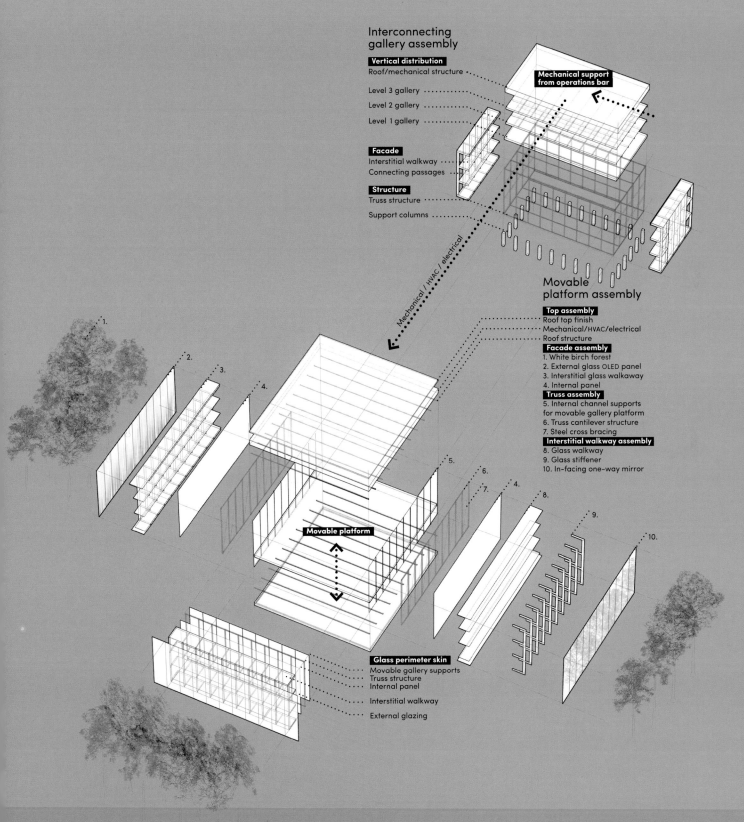

Interconnecting
gallery assembly

Vertical distribution
Roof/mechanical structure
Level 3 gallery
Level 2 gallery
Level 1 gallery

Facade
Interstitial walkway
Connecting passages

Structure
Truss structure
Support columns

**Mechanical support
from operations bar**

Mechanical / HVAC / electrical

Movable
platform assembly

Top assembly
Roof top finish
Mechanical/HVAC/electrical
Roof structure
Facade assembly
1. White birch forest
2. External glass OLED panel
3. Interstitial glass walkaway
4. Internal panel
Truss assembly
5. Internal channel supports
for movable gallery platform
6. Truss cantilever structure
7. Steel cross bracing
Interstitial walkway assembly
8. Glass walkway
9. Glass stiffener
10. In-facing one-way mirror

Movable platform

Glass perimeter skin
Movable gallery supports
Truss structure
Internal panel
Interstitial walkway
External glazing

Chapter 21

Nurai

Privacy and community created by a green architectural carpet.

A potential new developer client came to New York and we shared with them what we had shown Michael Shvo just a couple of months before: chairs, vases, other project ideas, and some crazy radical architectural concepts which we'd come up with. They said, "We like your way

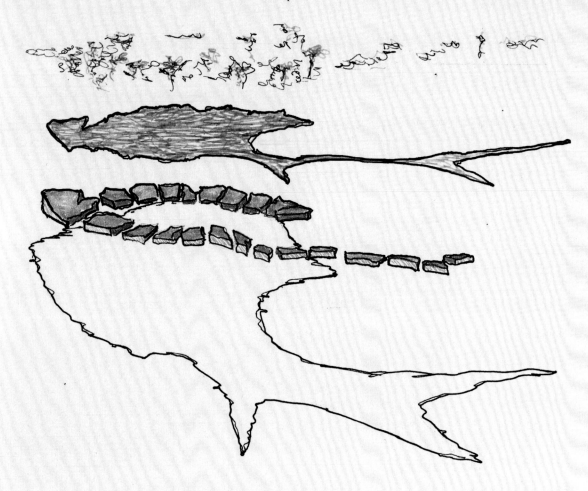

of thinking. We have 135,000 square meters of land off the coast of Abu Dhabi and we would like to create an island of high-end homes for clients that already have four, five, six homes around the world, as well as a hotel that would anchor them. Why don't you come up with an idea?" So they commissioned us for a conceptual study. I remember Michael calling me with this news on a Friday night. I was single, and by myself; I went to the bodega; I got a six-pack of Redbull and started an all-nighter, sketching at the apartment until 7 AM. I was just so excited that we got the commission.

The main questions that kept me busy were, "Why would anybody want to have an island house with neighbors if they already have five or six homes around the world? Wouldn't they buy their own island at that point? But then I considered that people do like to live with other people, they like communities, and they like the idea that there are people around them.

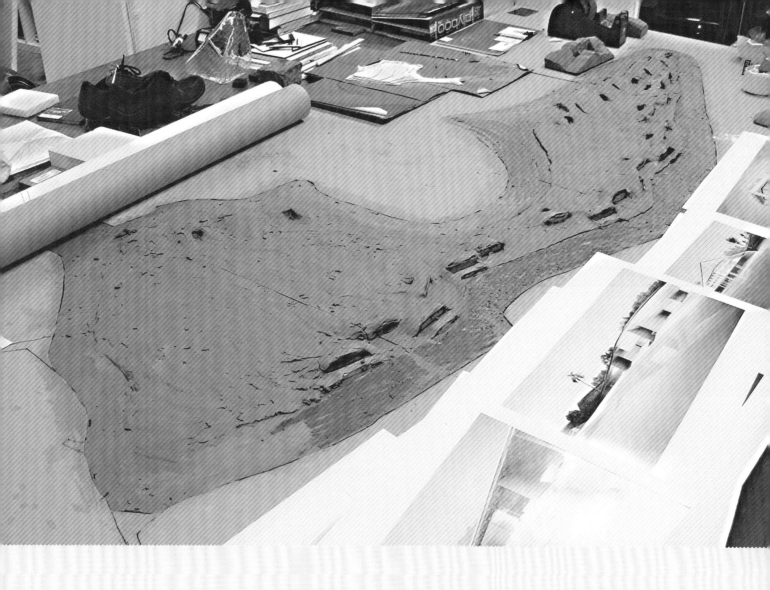

At the same time, they like their privacy. This tension between privacy versus luxury, community versus solitude, was what inspired me. How could we build a community on the island while simultaneously providing seclusion?

What I associated with the Persian Gulf was the ancient tradition of skillful carpet making. The thought of a floor covering prompted a compelling image in my mind. I thought about how when you ask kids to clean their room,

they'll shove their toys quickly under the carpet
to hide them. Even now, when we don't want to
see something, we have a very childish instinct
to hide the object beneath a rug. What if we had
a similar approach for this project? What if we
tucked everything that this island needs under a
green, vegetated carpet that covers the structures
so that when you are on the roof you can't see any
of the neighbors, but they're there? That was the
starting point, an idea of camouflaging, hiding,
blending urbanism into the natural landscape.

I began a sketch of a giant green architectural carpet over the island, tucking both residences and amenities that detract from the notion of solitude underneath. At first we looked at putting the houses all around the island and covering them with this carpet, with one structure in the middle covered with water, the pin holding the carpet down. We positioned each building in such a way that, from the roof, all the other structures are hidden by the continuous surface. The green carpet balances isolation with material comfort.

We created a very preliminary presentation for a masterplan that highlighted the hotel and residential components, and we sent it to Abu Dhabi after a little less than three months. We got a phone call back a few days later. I remember I was in a taxi coming back from the airport, it was December 2007, and they said, "We've shown your presentation to the Crown Prince Sheikh of Abu Dhabi and he wants to build it."

I was completely floored. At that point I didn't really know how to react so I just started laughing hysterically for what felt like minutes. The very serious people on the other side stayed quiet, waiting for me to relax, and when I did, I said, "Great, I have no idea how to build this." And they said: "We know, we've done our homework on the

size of your practice, the fact that you've never done any other project like this before, and we're willing to pad you with the knowledge that you're lacking." Another huge surprise, but for me it's one of the smartest things I've heard from a client because the fundamental thing that they cared about was the vision that we'd created.

Within a couple of weeks we were working with many specialists figuring out how to make this a reality. It was quite a surreal experience at first. A

lot of the people had areas of expertise we didn't even know how to pronounce at the time, but what really struck me was that the word "carpet" was being used in absolutely every meeting; the concept that I had first put forth was governing the approach for this project. Everyone around us was making that the essence and the core that the project fed from. And everyone recognized that our concept of the "green carpet" distinguishes and unifies the Nurai masterplan. The concept not only protected the integrity of the design, but also demonstrated the powerful impact of a holistic idea. We considered how we could utilize the gray water from the houses to water the vegetation, how to create the benefits from vegetation to shade the houses in that kind of climate. So in many ways the approach was also focused on being extremely sustainable.

At first I thought that we were lucky, we had no idea what we were doing. But at some point I realized that the healthiest approaches are not just those that make the most sense initially but also those that somehow continue to work logically in ways that are beneficial and most natural. Of course, unveiling that with the knowledge that specialists bring helps us gain that type of intelligence. In Nurai, we were able to question and innovate, unleashing value in ways that traditional ways of thinking may not have.

The masterplan features twelve waterside villas that complement twenty-four inland villas; each location had its own design typology. Oriented in alternating directions but adjacent to one another, the land residences zigzag throughout the site, all covered by a blanket of grass.

There were basically two main typologies for the land villas, which we called "Villa B" and "Villa F."

281

Villa B initially stood for "bachelor" and was later converted to "beach" because they were the ones closer to the beach. And Villa F stood for "forest" and later came to refer to "family."

Marked by its privileged views of the water, Villa B consists of two rectangular volumes, an orientation informed by traditional Arab living configurations. The structures are separated by an infinity pool and connected at the ground floor by a footbridge, which leads to a courtyard pool that reflects light onto the residence during the day. The beach-facing volume is an open, flexible space, while the other houses bedrooms, bathrooms, a kitchen, and other amenities over two floors.

Situated further away from the beach, Villa F is distanced from the water but is correspondingly less exposed, ensuring maximum privacy. Its entrance is on the second floor, creating dramatic views toward the horizon line, the front garden, and the courtyard. The villa's private and domestic spaces are divided between its two floors. Reflection pools at the perimeters give autonomy to the building's edges—a feature that paradoxically highlights the encroachment of the "green carpet."

The dozen bi-level water bungalows float like chandeliers from a structural frame above the

Persian Gulf. Residences are arranged corner-to-corner to maximize private views, and are preceded by pathways connected to a central pier.

At the time, the client proposed a ridiculously compressed timeframe. In December 2007 they said they wanted to open a sales office on the island in May of 2008. And I said, "Let me do a little research, I have no idea if this is possible." I called some of my architect friends and they said, "Dror, no. That's impossible. You can't open a sales office

in six months. You have to finish schematics, finish design drawings, then somebody needs to price the project, you need a preliminary budget, there will need to be some structural evaluation...You need about two and a half years." So I called the client back with that information and they said "Dror, we're going to support this project with knowledge that will allow us to open this project in May. We need you to help us to bring it to that point." And I said, "How are you even going to know how much these houses will cost?" And they said, "That's not

important. The price of those houses and the price of construction are negligible. If we create the right demand, we will be able."

So of course this was a very different kind of project. Normally you take those things into consideration and time is a necessity to create intelligent information prior to starting the project. But in this case, it wasn't important for them.

They did end up opening the sales office in May 2008. Once it opened, we didn't hear from them for a few days; we thought maybe sales were doing so-so. But three days later they called to say everything had sold out. The demand was so high that bidding wars began and at some point they just starting doubling the numbers for the price of the residences. Instead of reaching the goal, which was just below half a billion dollars, they collected $976 million worth of sales—breaking the record for the most expensive residential units sold in the United Arab Emirates per square foot at the time.

And as I sat in New York listening to this, I thought, This is better than any blockbuster movie that broke the record in its first weekend. If you put all of the projects that we'd done up until that time together, and added another zero you still wouldn't reach that kind of number. What did we do? What did we bring? What is the value we

create? What does this mean for our practice moving forward? And I think that for our studio this was the point where we really started to look at what we do and gained understanding about the value of an idea. It was the starting point for an ideas-driven design practice. The essence of what we created with Nurai was the idea. The project originally was supposed to be worth $154 million, but because of the composition of the "carpet" approach, they could build more residences onto the site.

We were less involved in the construction but the project is now complete. As an Israeli, I was unable to visit the UAE until I got an American passport. Just a couple of days after receiving my passport in 2014, Davina, our daughter Noï, and I went to visit the site. And honestly it was kind of weird stepping into a developed, finished project that just started as an idea seven years ago. Walking through the site, I was struck by the feeling of walking in a dream.

This project has a lot of meaning for me because, of course, it's our first built project, our first architectural project. We learned a lot about how we think and how we work and the values that we bring. We learned to work with specialists and gain the knowledge that we're lacking internally and how to set the stage for that work model.

....

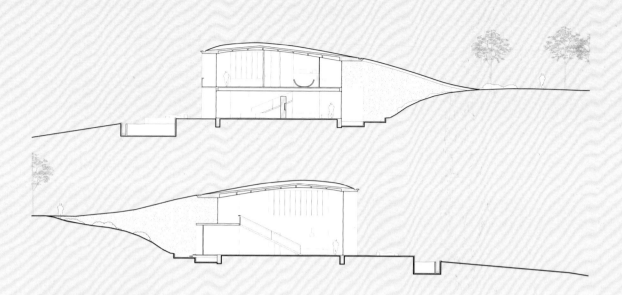

Beachfront Villa Type F

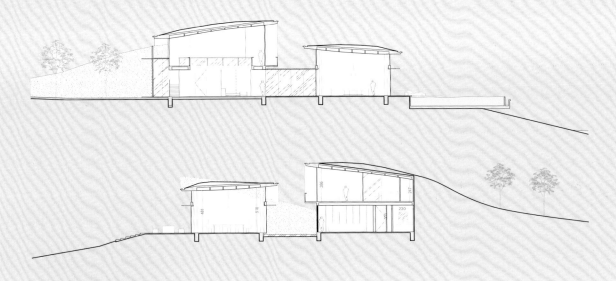

Beachfront Villa Type B

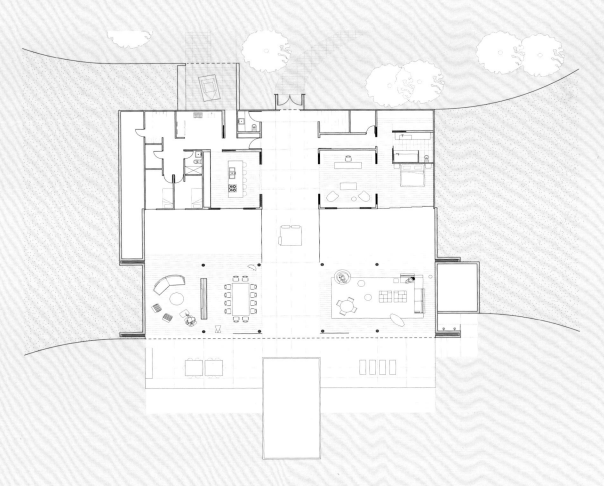

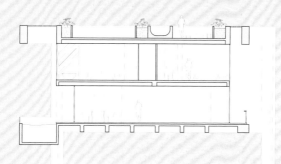

Water Bungalow

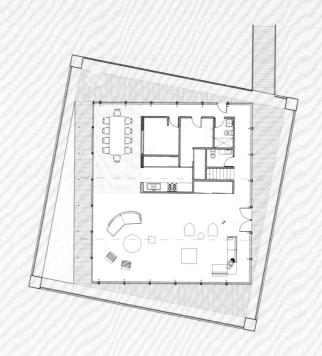

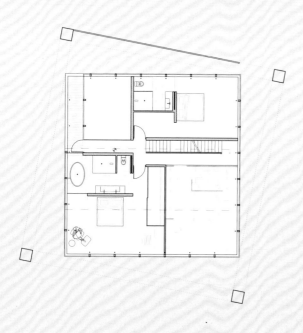

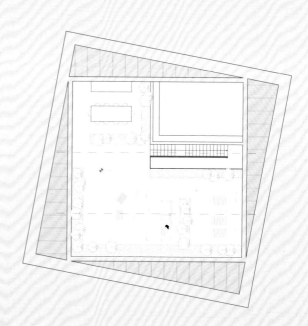

Porto Dubai

A slice of privacy.

After the commission of Nurai, the client asked us to look at another piece of land, this time in Dubai. They showed us a plot of land that was not an island but a circular peninsula, and they said: "We have a masterplan but we don't feel it's the right approach." After our first look at what they had, we thought: "Why is it organized it like a wedding cake?" The top was a skinny elevated piece, there was a wider elevated middle, and then below were houses directly on the beach.

We wondered if there was a way for us to create a masterplan that looks at this piece of land differently. Because it was almost round, the logical thing to us was, maybe instead of looking at it as a wedding cake, we look at it as a pie. The most natural way to cut a pie is to slice triangles. So we came up with a pie-shaped masterplan that mimics the clock face. You can imagine looking at a clock; in the peninsula

Porto Dubai

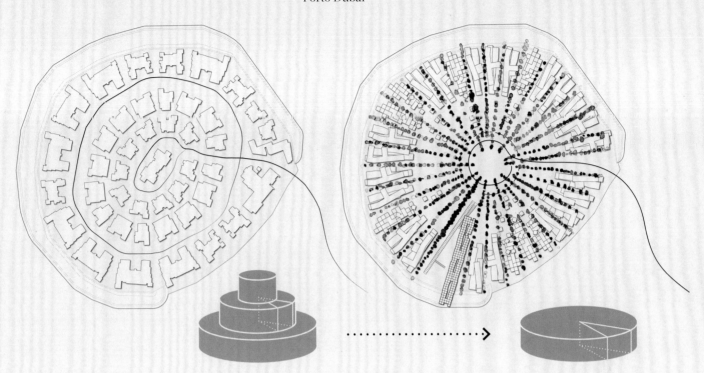

we created twelve different segments each with three houses so you can enter a vestibule at the center and gain entrance. The idea is that you first need to get to the center of the pie and from the center, each plot of land proceeds as a very skinny triangle, growing outwards. Every house enjoys a view on two sides. We separated the houses with a dense line of trees. So when you look back you see this density of trees in the center of the peninsula, and in extreme perspective every house has this very long garden that belongs to you and guides you in.

Each house is organized as a binocular that looks out to the horizon and into the garden from those two sides.

This organization has tremendous benefits for the utilization of the land. In terms of access, we conserved a larger percentage of land by orienting the access road directly to the center of the island and branching out radially from there, rather than having winding roads throughout. This approach preserves green space and maximizes efficiency and privacy with direct traffic routes.

....

Chapter 23
Hunters Hills

Can a neighborhood belong to a site?

The studio was invited to a closed competition for the creation of a new residential development on a site approximately 20 kilometers southeast of Prague.

Given the location's proximity to the Czech capital, I reasoned, its residents will likely work in the city but want to escape the bustle of urban life at home.

Instead of providing a typical suburban experience, I wanted to devise a new kind of living quarters that provided tranquility as well as community. To achieve this, I decided to create an authentic experience with nature—the ultimate retreat—by rethinking how public and private spaces relate to their surroundings.

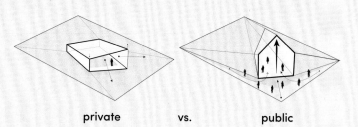

private   vs.   public

In studying the site, we realized that its undulating topography could be used as a tool for our architectural strategy: roadways and green roof-covered residences could be strategically arranged within the land's curves in a way that facilitated unobstructed views from every vantage point. Our masterplan for Hunters Hills ultimately utilized the staggered terrain in this way, where each residence is tucked into the landscape and oriented to maximize views based on its location. Instead of looking out onto clusters of buildings, all one sees is an oasis of lush vegetation.

Terraces, landscaping, and ample green space around each residence further produce harmony between structure and landscape. We created restaurants, a wellness center, school, hotel, and other structures based on this logic, plus seven typologies for houses, one of which is the Eco House (Chapter 14). As the only residence with a pitched roof, and

Hunters Hills

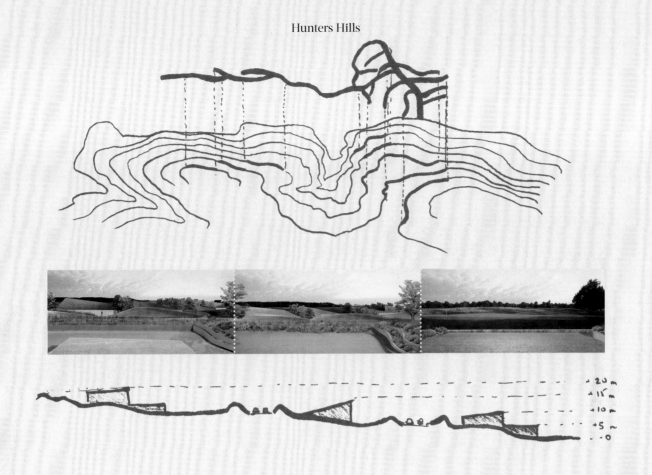

Seven housing typologies
with variety in yard landscaping and plot shapes

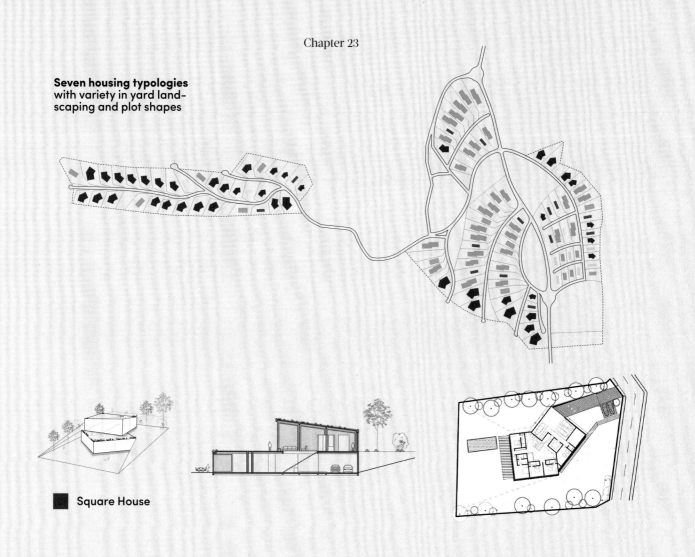

■ Square House

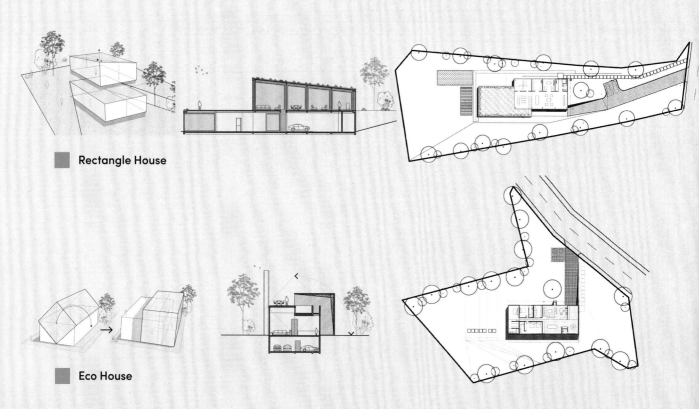

■ Rectangle House

■ Eco House

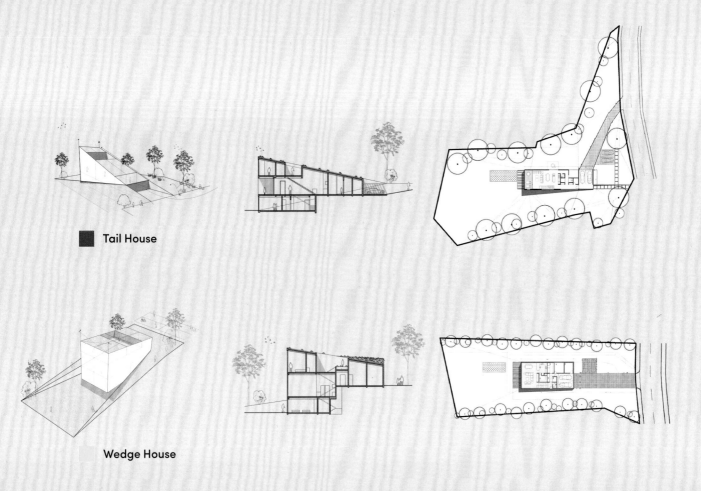

■ **Tail House**

Wedge House

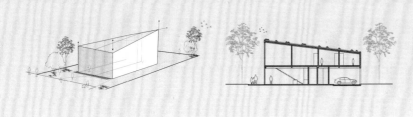

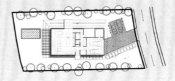

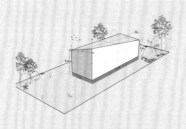

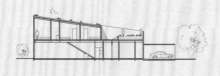

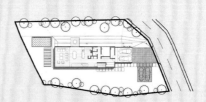

■ **Wide House**

■ **Long House**

therefore the only visible residence, the Eco House serves as a quiet sign of life amidst Hunters Hills' camouflaged built environment. Pitched roofs also cover commercial buildings, defining them as spaces for community and commerce rather than private dwellings.

Structures supplement the existing topography in our vision for Hunters Hills, transforming it into an extended landscape for living.

....

Hunters Hills

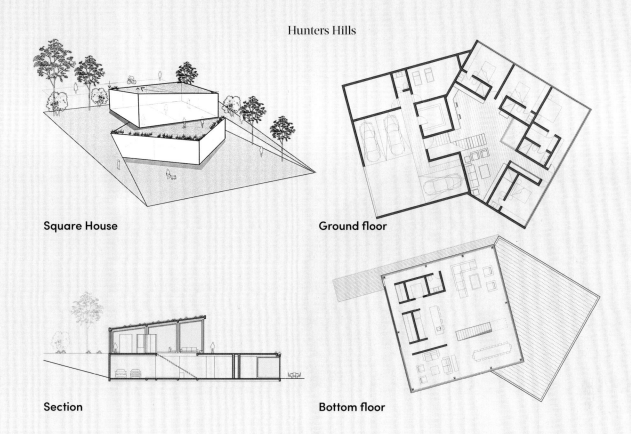

Square House

Ground floor

Section

Bottom floor

Hotel

Ground floor

Chapter 24

Havvada

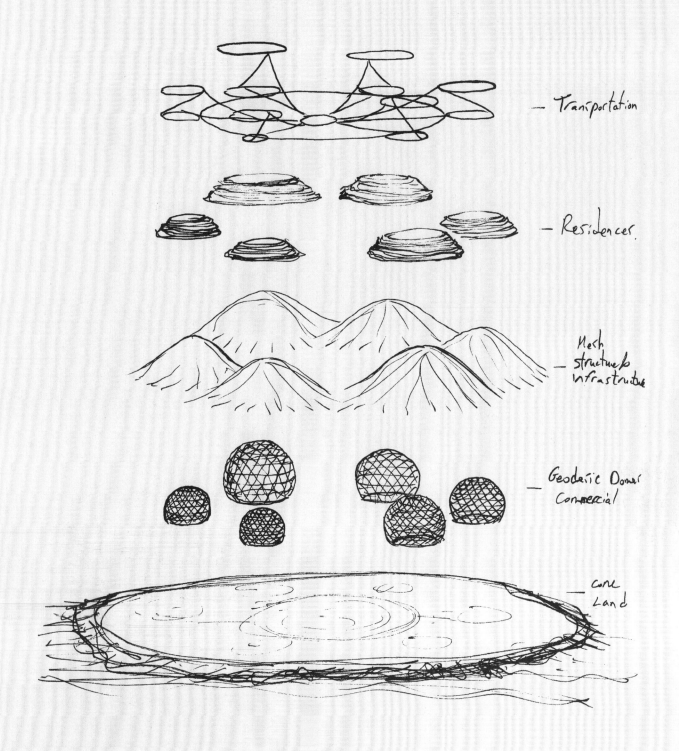

— Transportation

— Residences.

Mesh
structure/
Infrastructure

Geodesic Domes
Commercial

core
Land

A city of tomorrow that rethinks the urban grid.

This is a project that is very dear to me on many different levels. It's another one that starts with an interesting story. One day I received a phone call from a woman named Hale Haifawi in Istanbul saying, "Dror, I really like your work. I want to represent you in Turkey." And I said, "Ok, who are you? Who else do you represent?" And she said, "I don't represent anybody else. I want to represent you."

I responded, "I'm not looking for any additional representation, we are currently working with Culture and Commerce, and with CAA, but if you have any particular projects I'm very happy to hear about them." And she said "Listen, if you happen to come to Istanbul soon, let me introduce you to my beautiful city." I said, "Ok, sure." I came home and mentioned this to Davina; at the time we were actually planning to go to my sister's wedding in Israel a couple of months later and Davina said "Why don't we take a weekend in Istanbul right before?" I thought it was a good idea, why not.

So we planned for that and I sent Hale an email saying I would love to have coffee with her when I arrived in Istanbul. She responded, "Dror, please don't plan anything. Just come. Give me few days, I'm going to send you an itinerary, please let me take care of your stay."

And she sent me this very overwhelming itinerary. When Davina and I landed in Istanbul we were picked up directly from the plane by a black car on the tarmac. We skipped customs—to this day I have no idea how she did that—and went straight to a meeting with the mayor of Istanbul. There were gift exchanges, formal handshakes, and photographers...I was thinking, "Who is this lady and who does she think just arrived?"

We met with several more important people throughout the day up until midnight, when we ended

up at a developer's home. At some point, he raised his glass and said, "I have an announcement to make. I've been working on twenty visionary projects for the city of Istanbul. I have one more to go: twenty-one projects for the twenty-first century. I would like Dror to design it." I had no idea that an announcement like this would be made, and everybody started clapping. He started describing one of the projects that he's working on, which is the dredging of forty-six kilometers of Kanal Istanbul. This project would result in more than a billion cubic meters of soil that they don't know what to do with.

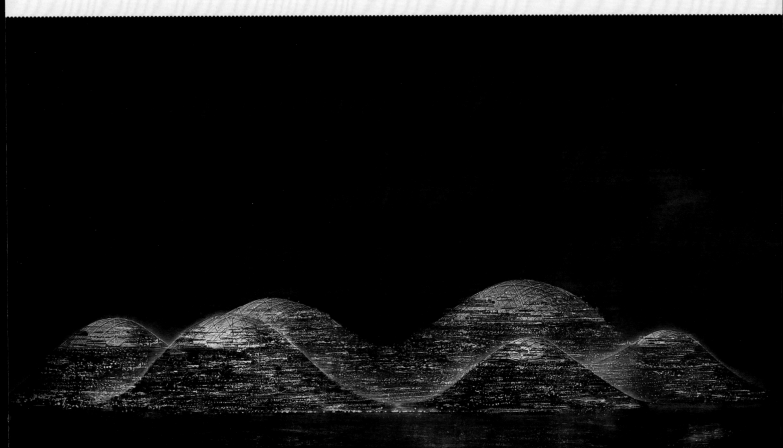

He wanted me to come up with an idea for what to do with all of that displaced soil. So I'm sitting there next to him and wondering what to say, how to respond... I felt as if a cow had landed on my plate and everyone shouted "Bon appetit!" Long story short, at 1 AM we were driving in a car back to his office for him to show us something on his computer. It was a surreal situation.

Later on we discovered that he, Davina and I all share the same birthday, March 13. He got very excited and said, "Ok, on March 13 we're going to debut this project."

And the date was set and the commission was announced and I went back to New York and said "Team, we have a very interesting challenge to work with."

At the time, the studio had never designed a project of this scale. We estimated that one billion cubic meters of soil would equate to an island of about three kilometers in diameter: approximately one-third the size of Manhattan if placed on the chosen site, which sits on a relatively shallow part of the Black Sea. If we could create an island from scratch,

what would we do? We started to think about
fundamental problems that have plagued modern
cities, as well as solutions posited to address them.
We considered urban planning, energy efficiency,
and advanced transportation systems, as well as
more basic questions: Why do we live in cities? What
is their purpose? Will cities exist in the future?

Every time I'd visited Istanbul, I was struck by its
quality of life and its surrounding dome-like hills. The
naturally elevated terrain allows all residents to enjoy

the horizon line. I wanted our design to give residents a similar perspective, as opposed to creating vertical buildings that obstruct views. From that first trip, Davina and I experienced the most amazing things of this city, and the most challenging, starting with traffic; standing in traffic for hours going from one meeting to the next. Just like a lot of cities, Istanbul also suffers from pollution, issues with garbage collection, crowded public transportation, and so on. So if we took a utopian approach, what should a brand new twenty-first century city look like?

At this point we were so fascinated by the project that we dove deeply into it, and we started generating ideas 24/7. We created something that I strongly believe in and that is not just interesting for this particular context in Turkey, but has potential for a lot of other places in the future.

We considered the problems resulting from the form and structure of modern cities: skyscrapers are stick-like buildings that plug into the grid, absorb energy, and emit waste. In our modern cities, structures don't contribute to each other, in fact, buildings take what they need from the grid and throw back what they don't. It's a selfish system, and with every new building someone's view gets blocked, and light is reduced.

Havvada envisions a new organization of the urban grid, where independent vertical structures on a 2D grid are rotated to form horizontal structures on a 3D grid; the structures wrap around the dome-shaped terrain in concentric circles.

Havvada is generated from two primary geometries: the triangle and the circle. These shapes present unique structural advantages apparent throughout the island, from its transportation grid to architectural frames. Each hill and dome is made of triangles; when these triangles overlap, they form the geometry of QuaDror. Buildings have QuaDror skeletons. This

Havvada

From 2D grid to 3D grid

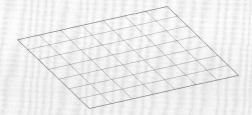 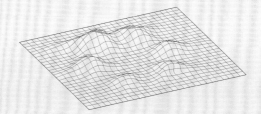

Meeting point of infrastructure and building
From independant buildings on a 2D grid

To horizontal buildings on a 3D grid

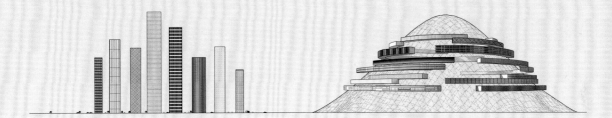

A new relationship between structure and infrastructure.

geometry allows for a very strong, lightweight frame that facilitates maximum light and unobstructed views of the horizon line.

The hill orientation of Havvada is rooted in a sacred geometry of the number seven, where six objects surround a central point. This configuration is apparent in nature, religion, physics, and even in the molecular shape of water. Havvada's organization is further informed by the study of chakras and Leonardo da Vinci's Vitruvian Man: each hill represents a different area of focus, which is housed at the heart of the dome and easily accessible via cable cars and the rapid transportation grid. These centers will feature districts for entertainment, education, sport, business, art, and a stadium.

We realized that turning a two-dimensional urban planning grid into a three-dimensional geographical typology generates major transportation benefits, including the accessibility to commercial centers from the surrounding hillsides. To get from one point to another, residents enjoy another benefit of a circular path: one can walk around it, or go straight across at every level.

We also drew from Buckminster Fuller's geodesic dome—a structure that has long fascinated us. Made of triangular units, the dome's form, Fuller argued, was twice as strong as typical rectangular houses; the hemispherical structure also encloses the maximum volume of interior space using the minimum amount of surface area, thereby significantly reducing cost. That volume also results in interior atmospheres that allow air to circulate more freely, so heating and

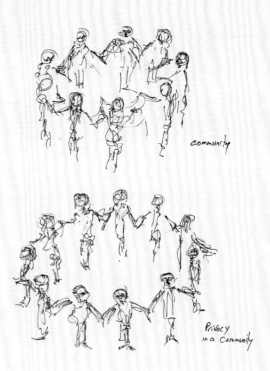

Community

Privacy
in a Community

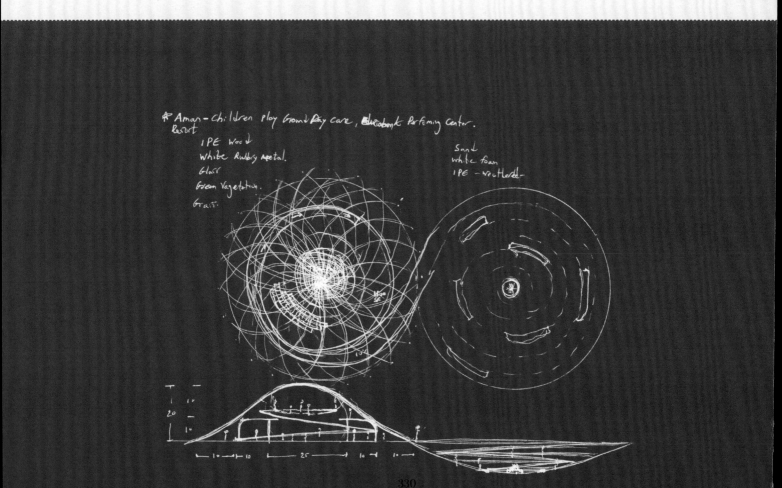

cooling occurs efficiently. By incorporating Fuller's logic of geodesic domes, each hill becomes a living machine. The form of the domes and green-roofed buildings contribute to an independent ecosystem and island-wide renewable/sustainable energy operations. Both wind and rain are recycled constantly.

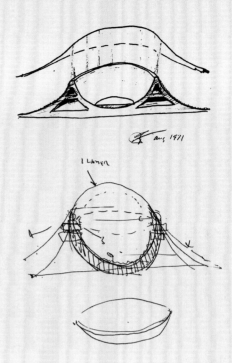

Old Man River's City
Buckminster Fuller

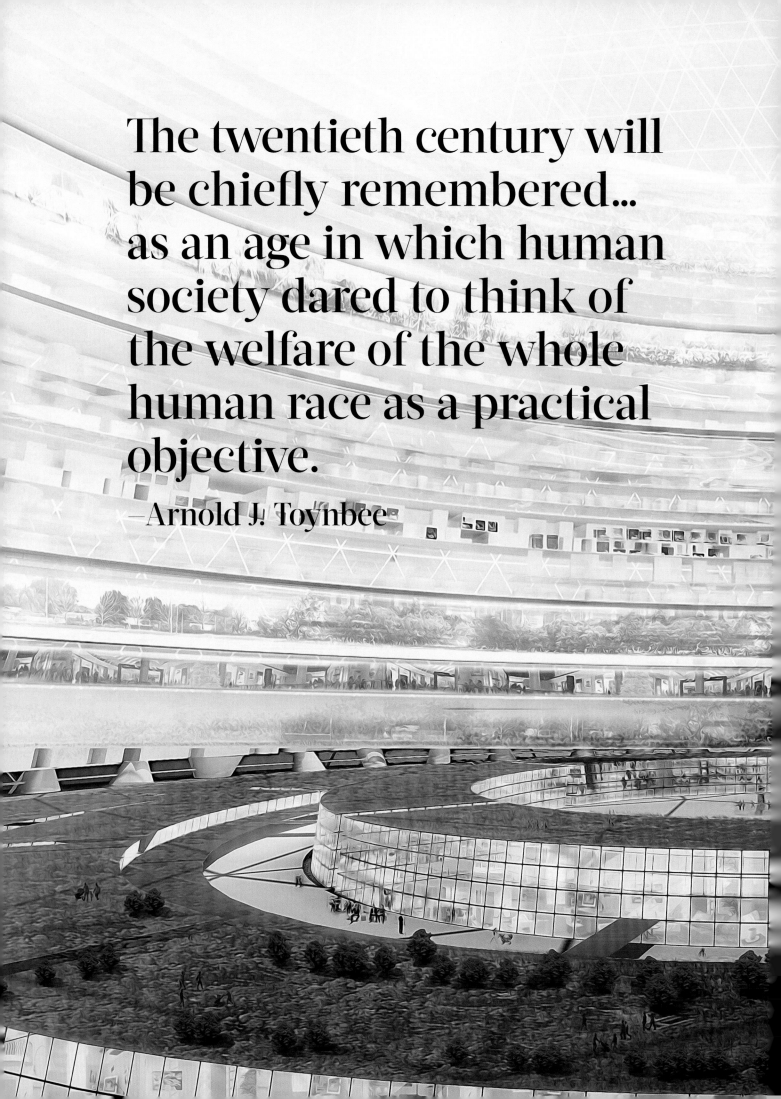

The twentieth century will be chiefly remembered... as an age in which human society dared to think of the welfare of the whole human race as a practical objective.

—Arnold J. Toynbee

Building heavy ≠ building strong
Mixing tension & compression

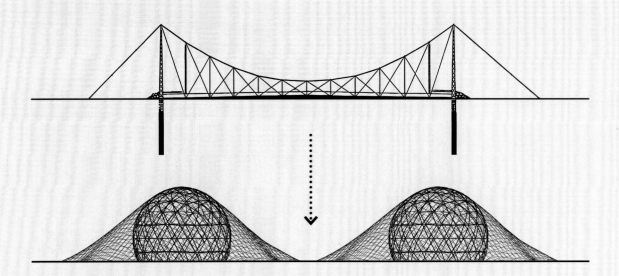

Total Area	Inhabitants		
16.535.000 m²			
11.574.500 m²	max. 385.600		30% void
8.267.500 m²	min. 275.000		50% void

Residential spaces

🌳🌳 Park

▬▬ Transportation

▱ 5m
to
▱ 20m unit height

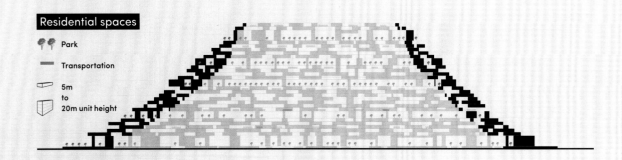

Commercial spaces

Havvada

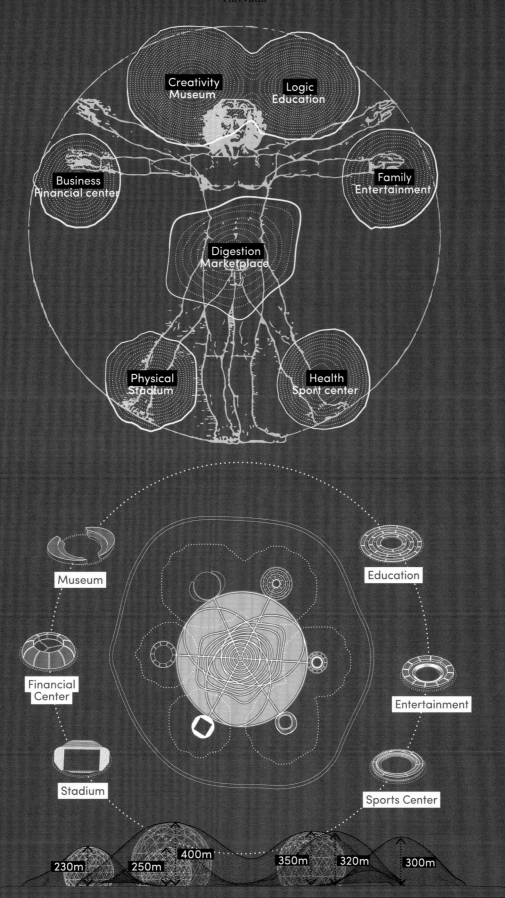

Creativity
Museum

Logic
Education

Business
Financial center

Family
Entertainment

Digestion
Marketplace

Physical
Stadium

Health
Sport center

Museum

Education

Financial
Center

Entertainment

Stadium

Sports Center

230m 250m 400m 350m 320m 300m

335

Chapter 24

Energy

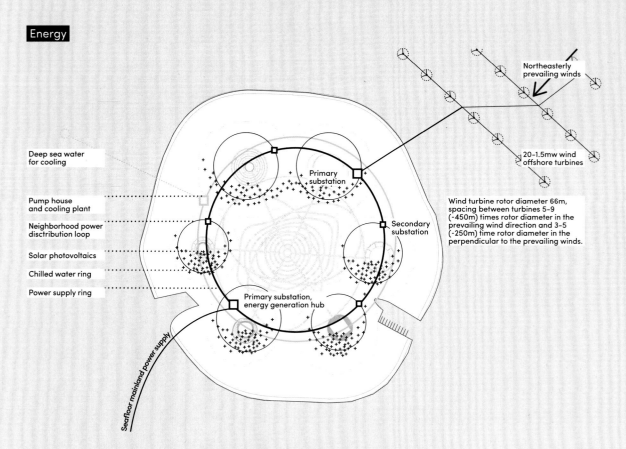

Deep sea water
for cooling

Pump house
and cooling plant

Neighborhood power
disctribution loop

Solar photovoltaics

Chilled water ring

Power supply ring

Primary
substation

Secondary
substation

Primary substation,
energy generation hub

Seafloor mainland power supply

Northeasterly
prevailing winds

20-1.5mw wind
offshore turbines

Wind turbine rotor diameter 66m,
spacing between turbines 5-9
(~450m) times rotor diameter in the
prevailing wind direction and 3-5
(~250m) time rotor diameter in the
perpendicular to the prevailing winds.

Water

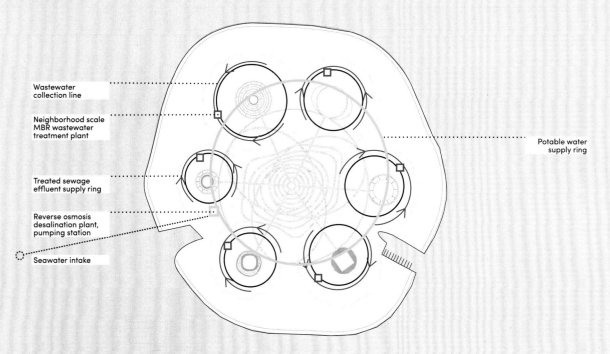

Wastewater
collection line

Neighborhood scale
MBR wastewater
treatment plant

Treated sewage
effluent supply ring

Reverse osmosis
desalination plant,
pumping station

Seawater intake

Potable water
supply ring

Waste

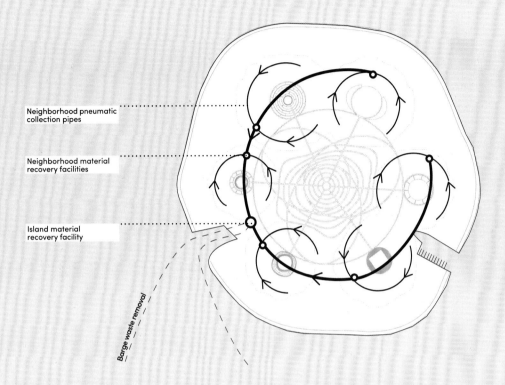

Neighborhood pneumatic
collection pipes

Neighborhood material
recovery facilities

Island material
recovery facility

Barge waste removal

Transportation

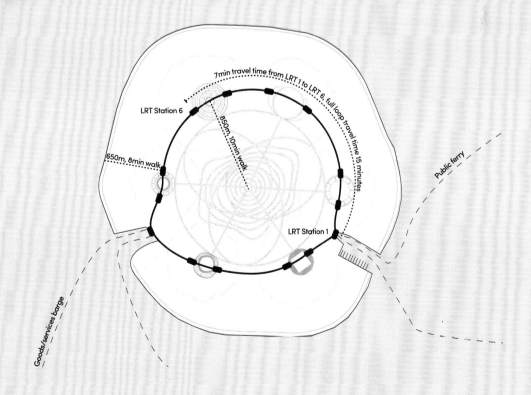

7min travel time from LRT 1 to LRT 6, full loop travel time 15 minutes

LRT Station 6

850m, 10min walk

650m, 8min walk

LRT Station 1

Public ferry

Goods/services barge

The steep slopes also contribute to the ventilation system. Agriculture can take advantage of each hill's microenvironment. To accomplish this, we needed to completely rethink the integration of the island's built environment and its terrain.

As we developed this project I flew to Japan to meet with Shoji Sadao of Fuller and Sadao PC Architects, the former director of the Isamu Noguchi Foundation and Buckminster Fuller's partner for over fifty years. I shared this project with him because I was interested in gaining insight into geodesic domes. He brought to my attention Old Man River's City, a massive urban project that Bucky proposed but never built. Sadao showed me some sketches that Bucky did in 1971 that looked very similar in logic to what I had just been sketching on the plane.

The studio spent six months in intense dialogue with a team of experts—aside from Sadao, Greg Otto and Byron Stigge of BuroHappold, Elizabeth Thompson and Daniel Reiser of the Buckminster Fuller Institute, Lisa Sardinas, and architects John Kuhtik and Joaquin Bonifaz—collaboratively researching and constantly ex-perimenting with ways to design an unprecedented, net-positive-energy, sustainable island. A new kind of city.

This approach with Havvada doesn't need to be in the Black Sea. It doesn't need to be in the water or be that particular size. It can have more than six radial hills to be something more concentrated, but communities created from aggregated units, and how dynamic structures can facilitate cohesive community life is very interesting to me, something that I definitely want to take to the next step at some point. I have some particular ideas in mind, and I could talk about this project for hours. This proposal represents a very inspiring idea. Havvada is a landscape that will continually adapt to the dynamics of its unique site. Its strategic topography and built environment creates a self-sufficient, ever-changing dual tension between the organ and the machine. We are currently developing this approach for other urbanistic challenges around the world.

Chapter 25

Parkorman

How can we make people fall in love with nature again?

The studio was commissioned to create a proposal for a park in Istanbul's Şişli district, located approximately six miles north of the city center within the sprawling Fatih Forest. Green spaces are few and far between in the Turkish metropolis—making the opportunity to design a central park there incredibly significant. We began researching the

history of major parks: many were designed more than a century ago, when the relationship between people and nature was more cohesive than it is today. Today when urban dwellers encounter large areas of nature—in a park, forest, mountainside, or otherwise—the unfamiliar environment can elicit anxiety, and even fear. The opposite of fear, we reasoned, is love. How could we make people fall in love with nature again?

We challenged ourselves to create a masterplan filled with conditions, or moments, to fall in love with a forest. The studio's goal was to create a context for people to experience the highest level of affection—unconditional love—through personal 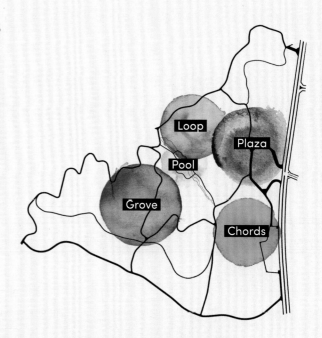 encounters with nature. We created a network of conditions that provoke unique experiences: accentuating and framing nature (feeling), using the forest as a stage for reflection and fantasy (imagining), encouraging interaction and play (doing), and presenting nature as a place for collective experience (sharing). Together, these experiences reintroduce nature to urban life.

Pollination:
the eros of nature.

As we thought about how people would use
the park—to play, meditate, converse, exercise,
read, or picnic—we wanted to create open-ended
conditions that encourage those activities. We
decided to design various non-linear paths and
environments: a living system of places for visitors
to explore. In this way, each person is empowered
to create his or her own experience, resulting in a
more intimate and memorable relationship with
the park.

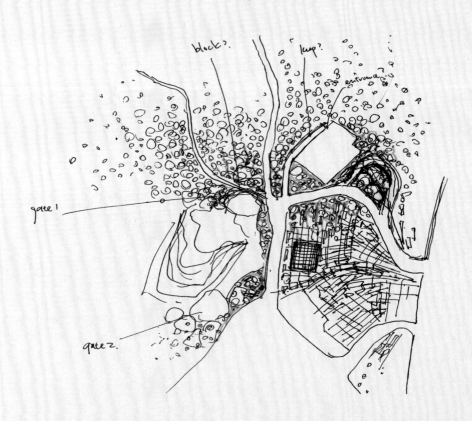

Our masterplan for Parkorman narrates a love story between people and nature. It consists of five main zones: the plaza, the loop, the chords, the pool, and the grove. Each has its own distinct qualities that foster conditions for this love.

We decided to empower visitors to explore nature at their own pace. Visitors to Parkorman enter via the plaza, which slowly puts nature center stage: geometric patches of concrete tile mimic the grid-like vocabulary of an urban landscape, allowing

for a comfortable transition from the city into the forest. As visitors move further into the park, the orientation of the grass and concrete flips, creating geometric green patches suitable for sitting or picnics. The grass ultimately forms quiet moments surrounded by earthen pathways. Nearby, a crescent-shaped hilltop—the highest point in the park—invites visitors to lounge on its stepped interior; a perfect circle of water lays at its center and gives way to a weaving running trail that snakes down the hillside. The concrete gradually disappears

Familiar urban forms slowly transition into organic moments deeper inside the forest.

completely, while the remaining greenery morphs into organic shapes, and the landscape progresses from a familiar urban landscape to nature.

Visitors choose how to navigate the park's trails: either from side-to-side along an elongated running path, or down the center, where a helix-shaped walkway of steps provides a shortcut directly through. Swings and hammocks hang from trees surrounding the winding path, providing a means for play or repose. At the hill's base, a playground comprising

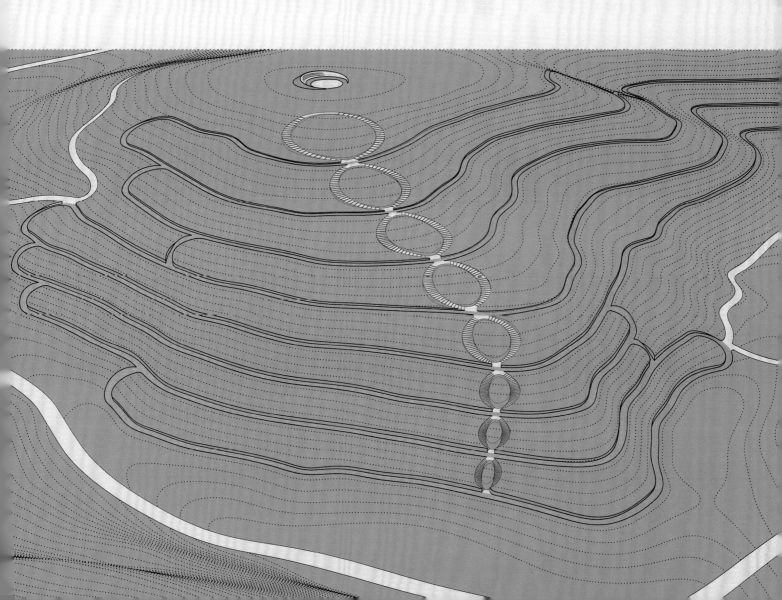

giant ball pits varying in depth and size (inspired by Turkish spice markets) sits along a wide canal.

The next environment is accessed by any one of seven distinct paths, each providing a different experience of walking in a forest. They intersect at a single point: the Fountain of Clarity. Conceived as a means for emotional cleansing, the fountain's cube-shaped frame sends a screen of water— a literal mirror for reflection—down all four sides. To enter the structure, the guest's approach triggers

a sensor that activates a hydraulic piston and forms a temporary opening. Surrounded by walls of water that hide the forest, one can look up at the open sky.

Another trail that leads to the fountain offers yet another experience of walking in a forest, where the footpath slowly rises above the ground, zigzagging around tree trunks to provide different perspectives of the foliage. As the path floats higher above the ground, it twists into giant loops—with trampolines at the center—that invite visitors

353

to change their movement from walking to jumping. Bounce on the highest trampoline to get a view of the treetops, just over the horizon line.

Beyond these pathways lies The Grove, a maze of trails that lead to a series of site-specific sculptures. Each will be commissioned pieces; in the images here we suggest works by Andy Goldsworthy, Anna Liu, Mike Tonkin, and Jaume Plensa. Every artwork and its surrounding landscape relates to each other, forming spirographic patterns when viewed from above: a sphere-shaped mass of wood is reached by a path of wood chips (Goldsworthy), as if it were rolled into place along the grass. A sound installation, formed by a hurricane-shaped tower of hollow rods, doubles as an organ fueled by the wind (Liu and Tonkin). The work is reached by a trail of loose pebbles, allowing visitors' footsteps to act as a second instrument as they walk along the path.

Parkorman's many environments, approved by the municipality, yield a multitude of paths that highlight the richness of the forest. Through its experience-focused masterplan, the park empowers visitors to author their own adventure.

....

Proposed installation
Tonkin Liu

Proposed installation
Jaume Plensa

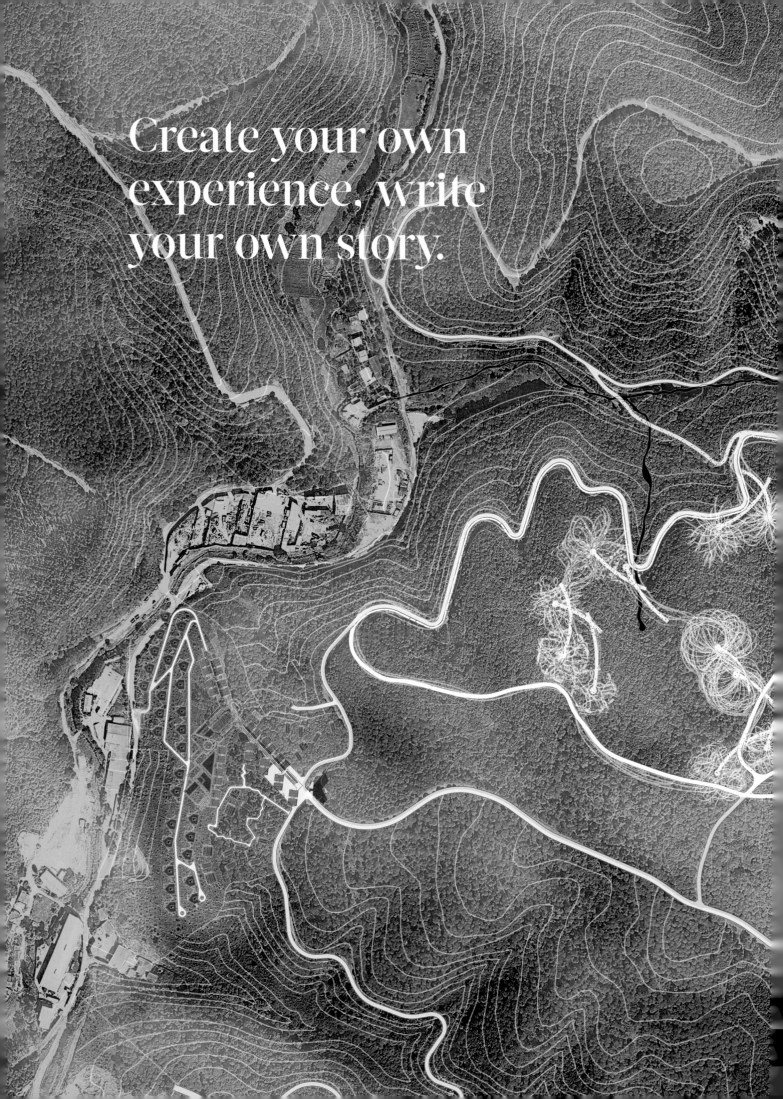

Create your own
experience, write
your own story.

Chapter 26
Galata Grounds

A new neighborhood embraces the history and culture of Istanbul.

This is one of the biggest, most exciting endeavors we've ever worked on. It started when our Director of Architectural Design, Christine Djerrahian, and I presented the Parkorman project in Istanbul, which was extremely well received. We were aware that the same client had acquired a large piece of land on the edge of Karakoy, facing the Old Town across

Returning 1.2km of boardwalk to the people of Istanbul

the Bosphorus, and we were curious to know what this project was all about, so we asked. The first reaction we got was, "Dror, forget about it. It's not for you. It's a really big project and we're looking at some big firms such as SOM, HOK, Herzog & de Meuron. You're too small." So then we were even more curious and we asked more questions until the client said, "You know what? Let me send the CEO of the project with you tomorrow morning to take a look at the land." We said, "Yes, we would love to tour it and also see the brief you've sent to those other firms."

The Galata Port project, a post-industrial area located in the up-and-coming neighborhood of Karaköy, is one of the most important developments in the city's rapidly changing architectural landscape. It encompasses two distinct waterfronts, the historical Karaköy Quay and the modern Salıpazarı Quay, and connects an intricate web of cultural and historical landmarks, one of which is the Istanbul Modern.

When we returned to New York, all we could think of was that they were stuck with this idea that our studio

was too small to take this on, and what could we do about it? At that time we had started a dialogue with Gensler about another project and said, "Well, Gensler is the biggest, we are very small; maybe we can team up? Maybe the client can benefit from the best of both worlds? A small, innovative studio and big, extremely capable company." We asked Gensler if they would be interested in partnering on this submittal and they said yes. We called the client and asked them if they were willing to add us as a sixth entry for this competition and they said sure.

Our first realization was that the project was really massive and intimidating, even to the client itself. We felt the need to somehow shrink the project conceptually in their minds so they could understand certain motivations. When we toured the site there were a lot of historical buildings that weren't going anywhere. Some were landmarked buildings, but not in good shape, in need of restoration. The analogy we had in our mind was: "Imagine they are teapots that need to be restored and polished. What would you do to give them more respect, a

stronger presence?" And we thought: "The tray. Let's put all of the restored, polished pots on top of a beautiful silver tray." We started to play with this idea of *landmarking* as a physical process: marking the land. When you walk into a mosque, you step on their beautiful carpets, you change your pace, you pay attention, and you're more respectful. It's the same for any other grounds you walk on; if you feel it's more beautiful, better designed, you actually give it a heightened attention. So this was the starting point for us.

Second, we realized that half of the site was contracted to be the largest cruise ship terminal in Istanbul for another ten years, so it was closed off to any other primary use. How were we going to accommodate the needs of a cruise ship operation while making this a beautiful neighborhood for pedestrians to enjoy?

This led to the most important idea that we invested in this project: solving that conundrum by taking the infrastructural needs of the docked cruise ships and burying them underground. We brought our focus to the boardwalk. The ships have to dock right in front of the most important and valuable part of the site: 1.2 km of Bosphorus waterfront. Together with BEA Architects, a consultant brought on board to address the port's functions, we wondered, "Can the boardwalk itself lift up hydraulically in order to create a secure zone around the ship? Hydraulic gangways could rise from underground to pick up the passengers and take them straight to a basement level where all embarking and disembarking needs are accommodated. By placing arrivals and immigration, duty free, luggage claim, and connections to civic transportation (buses and taxis) under the boardwalk, cruise ship passengers could use the site without affecting the pedestrian flow at ground level. This innovative approach—as much a product design solution as an urban planning one—really appealed to the client and we were awarded the project and designed the masterplan.

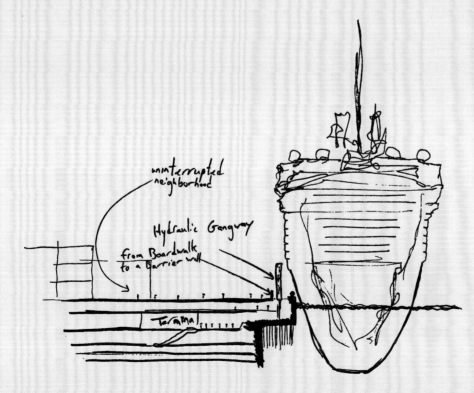

uninterrupted
neighborhood

Hydraulic Gangway

from Boardwalk
to a Barrier wall

Terminal

Kılıç Ali Paşa
Mosque

Tophane
Fountain

To[...]
Pa[...]

Nu[...]
Tow[...]

Terminal/Parking

Istanbul
Modern
Museum

Karaköy Quay   Salıpazarı Quay

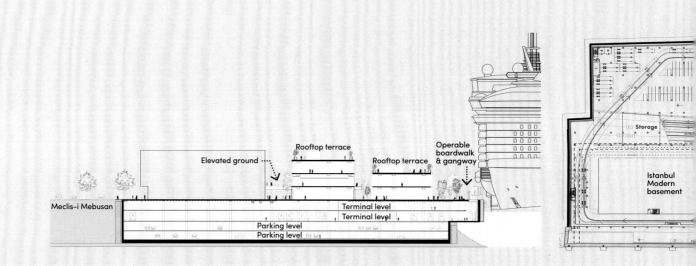

Meclis-i Mebusan

Elevated ground

Rooftop terrace

Rooftop terrace

Operable
boardwalk
& gangway

Terminal level
Terminal level

Parking level
Parking level

Storage

Istanbul
Modern
basement

376

Nusretiye
Mosque

Terminal/Parking

Mimar
Sinan
University

Old City Viewport

...raulic Boardwalk

Shopping Street · Courtyard · Water Square · Old City View

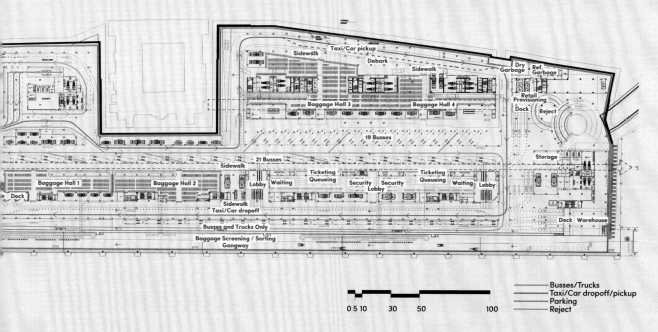

Taxi/Car pickup

Sidewalk

Debark

Sidewalk

Dry
Garbage

Ref.
Garbage

Retail
Provisioning

Dock

Reject

Baggage Hall 3

Baggage Hall 4

19 Busses

Storage

21 Busses

Sidewalk

Baggage Hall 1

Baggage Hall 2

Lobby

Waiting

Ticketing
Queueing

Security
Lobby

Security

Ticketing
Queueing

Waiting

Lobby

Dock

Dock

Warehouse

Sidewalk
Taxi/Car dropoff

Busses and Trucks Only

Baggage Screening / Sorting
Gangway

0 5 10   30   50   100

Busses/Trucks
Taxi/Car dropoff/pickup
Parking
Reject

377

Tradition is always a rewriting, a reinvention.
–Antoine Picon

"View of Tophane Karakoy"
Jean-Baptiste Hilaire

Textured

Smooth

Warm

Lush

The city of Istanbul takes advantage of its scenic setting and climate; a lot of city life is lived in outdoor spaces. We wanted to preserve and honor that relationship by looking at each building in the masterplan as a pedestal, creating beautiful outdoor rooftops. When we understood this was key, we shifted from calling this project Galata Port to Galata Grounds; the emphasis is no longer at the strait but instead in the renewed access to and usage of the site by the community. The idea was to create something that takes from the existing culture and reinvents it.

In the masterplan, public spaces are woven together with buildings with cultural, retail, office, and hospitality uses. The beautiful complexity is generated by simple gestures; breaking up the existing program into a collection of smaller buildings, carefully organized to extend the urban experience and connect the city to the water.

With the goal of revitalizing the identity of this area while paying homage to the site's history and context, the project rests on three guiding principles: respect, surprise, and harmony. The masterplan invites visitors from all over Istanbul and the world to experience something new and eclectic—yet familiar.

Holland Park

Blanketing a traffic node with a park that picks you up.

This project started from an invitation to think about 100 Varick Street, a site that faces the entrance to the Holland Tunnel—a notoriously gridlocked gateway out of New York City that opens up to three major highways on the New Jersey side. On one hand it's a great location: one minute from Soho, from Tribeca, from the waterfront....

On the other hand, you're facing one of the most polluted, noisy, and congested areas of Manhattan. When we met with the zoning attorney he said that the city was very welcoming of art in this part of New York because they wanted to attract more residential development. But what did that mean? He said, "Come up with some ideas. We'll see."

So the first thing we thought was, "What if we create this massive awning that covers Varick Street and the and the traffic around the Freeman Plaza intersection?

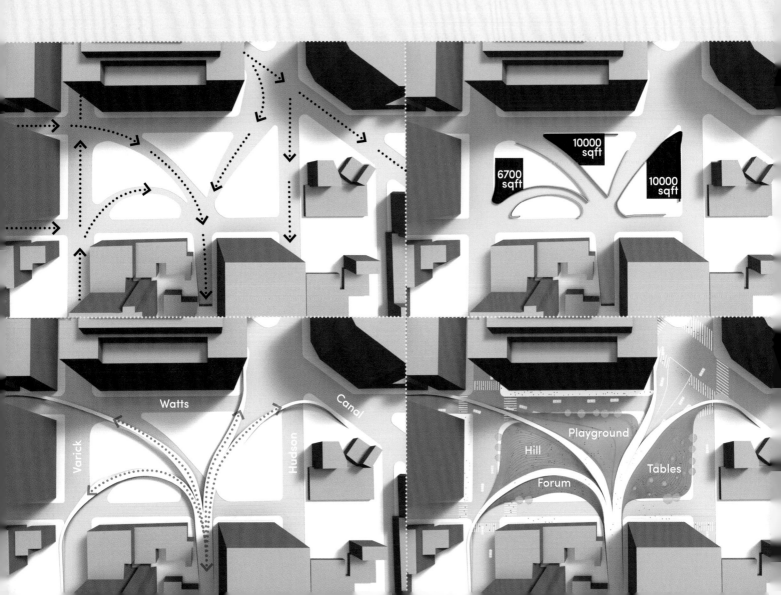

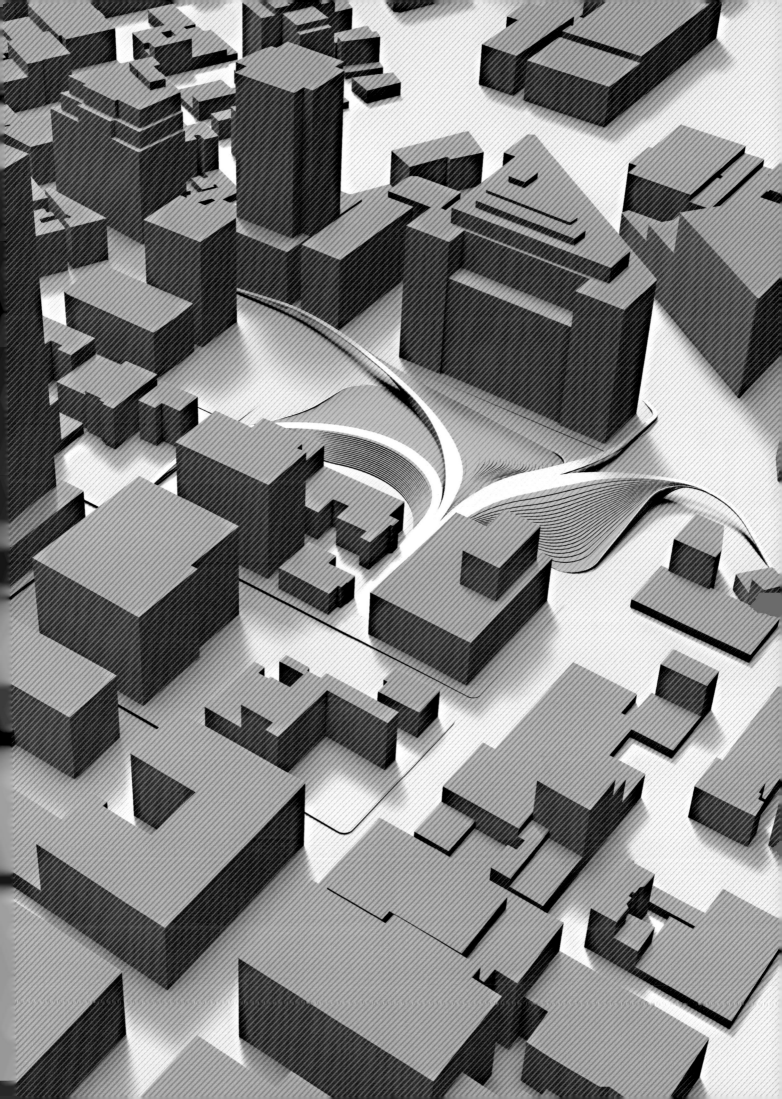

What if there was a vegetated canopy that blocks the view of the road from the apartments above and reduces the noise and pollution a little bit?" When the developers saw the canopy concept they said, "Well why don't you cover all of Freeman Plaza that adjoins Varick Street?"

We imagined being plucked from the chaos of the city and transported into a green oasis. To make this dream a reality, we designed a living, breathing barrier: a public park that elevates pedestrians,

both literally and figuratively, above one of the most hectic exit nodes in Manhattan.

We used the existing forms of the streets to create environments for different activities that take advantage of the landscape.

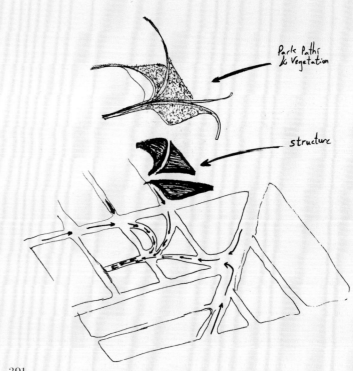

Park Paths & Vegetation

structure

391

Inspired by the sinuous flows of traffic into the mouth of the tunnel, our concept for Holland Park creates a unique space that drapes over its surroundings like three leaves. Eliminating dangerous pedestrian crossings and traffic interruptions, the gentle ramps lift visitors from the street and carry them into the heart of the park. The idea of hosting the bustle underneath was quite interesting to us because at the time we worked in this neighborhood; we also crave places to have lunch and places that transport us

out of work mode and the city. So the idea was to create a gathering place for groups to enjoy the neighborhood at all times.

Looking at the park, it's just like New York: open 24/7, with the potential for all kinds of activity, day or night.

....

Plucked from the chaos of the city and transported into a green oasis.

Rethink
Research
Reimagine
Redefine
Realize

Question everything!

———

Acknowledgments

I am eternally grateful to all of the people who have contributed to Studio Dror over the last seventeen years. The talent, dedication, personalities and perspectives you've brought has shaped the direction of my work, and the course of my path along the way. Seeing our ideas come to life is a gift. To all of the individuals below, thank you.

Drew Aaron
Linsen Abdon
Siddhant Agarwal
Sarah Alwen
Eirini Anthouli
Alvaro Arias
Bryson Armstrong
Nepal Asatthawasi
Leila Atlassi
Alex Auriema
Pola Bamberg
Zachary Bark
Dorin Baul
Nicolas Bazzani
Steve Becker
Ernst van ter Beek
Chloé Benchetrit
Ricardo Bojorquez
Matteo Bonacina
Joaquin Bonifaz
Julia Böttcher
Joey Bowers
Jan Brauer
Rachel Brooks
Robert Brown
Val Brown
Jo Burton
Josh Camarena
Francesco Caramella
Chad Carpenter
Daniel Chang
Leo Chao
Steve Chen
Ken Chiang
Dasom Choe
Ho Chi Choi
Junho Choi
Carol Chung
Evan Clabots
Alexandra Compton
Brandon Cook
Thomas Cook
Christine Corey
Melanie Courbet

Rozenn Couturier
Jean Couvreur
Robert Cox
Alexander Crean
Arielle Cruz
Corinne Cuozzo
Rob Dalton
Constance Delaux
Elena Delsignore
Gayatri Desai
Jordan Diatlo
Ian Diesendruck
Friso Dijkstra
Kaylie Dimock
Christine Djerrahian
Edward Dumpe
Noam Dvir
Brad Engelsman
Yasemin Etikan
Sylvia Feichtinger
Junyao Feng
Boback Firoozbakht
Julien Fuentes
Jess Fügler
Kanako Fukuda
Kajal Gala
Russell Greenberg
Soaib Grewal
Chester Griët
Merve Gulay
Mandy Han
Tim Torp Hansen
Stephanie Harroch
Romi Hefetz
Kaeo Helder
Renata Hermanny
Joa Herrenknecht
Karl-Johan Hjerling
Sam Ho
Minchul Hong
Ben Howes
Andy Hsu
Stephen Huang
Johan Hübinette

Geoff Hunt
Christian Igel
Melanie Iten
Alexandra Jenal
Taehyun Jeon
Tiffany Jow
Tim Karoleff
James Ian Killinger
Jae Woun Kim
Eileen Kiyonaga
Feyza Köksal
Broni Kotzen
Elisabeth Krenkler
Amity Kurt
Christina Kwak
Carson Lai
Karin Larsson
Eun Lee
Goldy Lee
Seongyong Lee
Casey Lewis
Gwenael Lewis
Lynn Lim
May Liu
Jillian Lockwood
Mario Martínez López
Mircea Masserini
Alice McGinty
Katie Merritt
Antonio Meze
Yilo Miao
Stephanie Micci
Irom Mimaroglu
Guy Mishaly
Tomoko Mori
Jason Neufeld
Adi Neumann Yehiel
Martin Nichols
Andra Nicolescu
Mina Onar
Mihoko Ouchi
Nicholas Oxley
Mehmet Özdemir
Luis Felipe Paris

Jung Soo Park
Harry Payne
Michael Peguero
Natascha Picard
Rui Pinho
Tanya Privé
Ben Raemer
Mark Reigelman
Benzi Rodman
Hamutal Ron
Davina Rosenbaum
Joey Roth
Luisa Ruge
Joyce Saiete
Aaron Saxton
Laura Schälchli
Verena Schreppel
Clara Schweers
Drew Seyl
Steven Shimamoto
Carrie Solomon
Alex Soss
Simon Spagnoletti
Shea Springer
Elias Stern
Kyle Stover
Kaitlyn Thornton
Aline Tom
Lyndon Treacy
Loukia Tsafoulia
Alvaro Uribe
Marieke Verkoelen
Zach Weiss
Karin Widmark
Reed Wilson
Eylül Wintermeyer
Shuman Wu
Jialun Wu
Yuchen Xiang
Dongfang Xie
Peter Xu
Thomas Yu
LiiLii Zhao
Bohan Zhang

Image credits

Alchemy Architects	205 (r)
Boffi SpA	61
David Chipperfield	380 (btm mid)
DBOX	158, 159
Adrian Fisk	175 (btm)
Martyn Gallina-Jones	132, 135
Darrin Haddad	163
John M. Hall	126, 130, 131
Tom Hayes	226, 227
Tony Hisgett	110 (top r)
Horm Italia Srl	172, 173, 202
Jessica Jones for	
Brancott Estate	front cover (btm), 2, 228, 229 (btm), 230, 399
Dan Keinan	128 (btm)
Jordan Kleinman	46, 50, 52, 55, 56, 57
Saverio Lombardi Vallauri	190
Ms Melina	76
Mustafa Nazif Duran	320
Utku Pekli	367 (top)
Gert Jan van Rooij	182, 195 (btm)
Isaac Rosenthal	108, 110 (btm rw), 111, 114, 115
Rosenthal GmbH	28, 30, 32
Erez Sabag	35, 42, 58, 59, 79, 81, 82, 85, 87, 92, 94, 96, 97, 99, 100, 101, 102, 103, 104, 106, 107
Ornella Sancassani	91
Studio EIS	278, 281
Leandro Texeira	197 (top r), 198, 200, 201
Sezgin Yilmaz	380 (top r)
Andrew Zuckerman	back cover, 22, 24

Every reasonable effort has been made to acknowledge the ownership of material included in this book. Any errors that may have occurred are inadvertent, and will be corrected in subsequent editions provided notification is sent in writing to the publisher.

Foreword © 2019 Aric Chen
Copyright © 2019 Studio Dror

Written by Dror Benshetrit and Alexandra Compton,
with contributions by Tiffany Jow and Luis Felipe Paris.
Edited by Alexandra Compton.

Library of Congress Control Number: 2019938085

ISBN 978-1-58093-521-0

10 9 8 7 6 5 4 3 2 1

Printed in China

The Monacelli Press
6 West 18th Street
New York, New York 10011

www.monacellipress.com